Pre-Raphaelite Drawings
in the British Museum

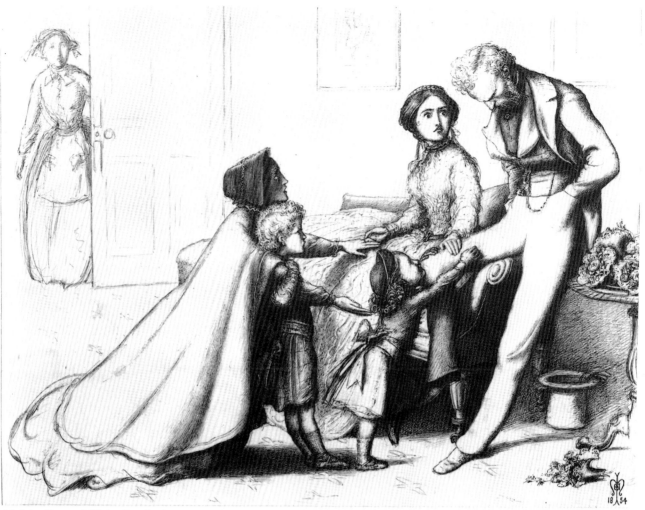

44 John Everett Millais: 'Retribution'

Pre-Raphaelite Drawings

in the British Museum

J. A. Gere

Published for the
Trustees of the British Museum
by British Museum Press

© 1994 Trustees of the British Museum

Published by British Museum Press
A division of British Museum Publications Ltd
46 Bloomsbury Street
London WC1B 3QQ

A catalogue record for this book is available
from the British Library

ISBN 0–7141–2603–9

Designed by James Shurmer

Typeset by Rowland Phototypesetting Ltd
Bury St Edmunds, Suffolk

Printed in Great Britain by BAS Printers,
Over Wallop, Hants

Contents

Introduction

Traditionally, 1848 is 'The Year of Revolutions'; and in September of that year three Royal Academy students started a revolution of their own by forming the Pre-Raphaelite Brotherhood: William Holman Hunt, Dante Gabriel Rossetti and John Everett Millais, aged respectively twenty-one, twenty and nineteen. They chose the name, in preference to 'Early Christian', as an expression of youthful impatience with the idealised 'Grand Style' derived from High Renaissance practice in general and from Raphael in particular. It emphasises Raphael's historical significance, but their actual knowledge of him, and indeed of any earlier Italian art, was derived almost wholly from engravings. In fact, the Pre-Raphaelite technique of detailed painting in transparent colour over a 'wet white' ground was of Flemish rather than Italian fifteenth-century inspiration. Jan van Eyck's *Arnolfini and his Wife* had been acquired by the National Gallery in 1842 and his *Man in a Turban* in 1851; and in 1849, when Hunt and Rossetti visited France and Belgium, Rossetti reported from Bruges 'the best of all are the miraculous works of Memling and Van Eyck'. But their taste was not exclusively for the fifteenth century. In Paris they admired Fra Angelico's *Coronation of the Virgin* in the Louvre, but were particularly struck by Ippolite Flandrin and by Paul Delaroche, whose *Children of Edward IV* ('The Princes in the Tower'), though painted in 1830, might be mistaken for a Pre-Raphaelite work of the early 1850s.

There were in all seven Brethren. Of the other four, Thomas Woolner did his best to express the ideals of the movement in his sculpture, so far as the medium allowed; James Collinson soon resigned, finding his religious convictions incompatible with membership; Frederick George Stephens produced a few pictures, of which *Mother and Child* (Tate) is the best known, but an over-fastidious critical faculty led him to abandon painting for art-criticism; Rossetti's younger brother William Michael was a conscientious chronicler of the activities of the PRB as a whole, and of his brother's life and work, but his ambitions were literary, not artistic. Effectively, the Brotherhood was a triumvirate.

Pre-Raphaelitism was a movement wholly English in origin and inspiration. It is possible to point to parallels elsewhere, notably the German 'Early Christian' or 'Nazarene' group active in Rome in the 1820s, but the fusion of High Seriousness, preoccupation with moral dilemmas, and absolute truth to nature which is the essence of Pre-Raphaelite art has a particularly English Protestant flavour. Every artistic revolution begins as a restatement of 'truth' – as the revolutionaries perceive it. The Pre-Raphaelites rejected the concept of generalised 'ideal' form. Truth to nature was a moral imperative. Every detail in a painting must be copied directly and precisely from nature (in his painting of *Christ in the House of his Parents* of 1850, now in the Tate

Gallery, Millais went so far as to use a carpenter as model for St Joseph, to ensure that the development of the arm muscles was correctly represented). A picture should edify by illustrating some moral truth, preferably in a contemporary context, and much ingenuity was devoted to devising subjects that should be more than mere anecdotes. Sometimes, as in Hunt's *The Hireling Shepherd* and *The Scapegoat*, the moral cannot be understood without an elaborate verbal explanation.

Of the founder-members, only Hunt remained faithful to these ideals. Three temperamentally more dissimilar people can seldom have combined in an artistic purpose, but each supplied qualities that the others lacked. Millais' prodigious technical brilliance and exquisite taste and, as his later work reveals, a certain superficiality of mind, were complemented by the passionate moral sincerity which transforms Hunt's sometimes clumsy and charmless execution; while Rossetti, whose relatively scanty technical resources were out of scale with his intellectual and imaginative power, inspired the others with something of his own poetic intensity.

Pre-Raphaelitism was not confined to the Pre-Raphaelite Brotherhood. Ford Madox Brown, born in 1821 and thus some years older than the others, had been a friend of Rossetti since 1847. He was never formally a member of the Brotherhood – no doubt he was felt to be too senior to be invited to join a students' society – but in 1850 he was a contributor to the Pre-Raphaelite journal, *The Germ* (see no. 38), and his paintings of the early and middle 1850s are entirely Pre-Raphaelite in technique and sentiment. So too are those of the tragically short-lived Walter Deverell (1827–1854), the best known of which is *The Pet* (or *A Lady Feeding a Bird*) in the Tate Gallery (see Mary Lutyens in *Pre-Raphaelite Papers*, Tate Gallery, 1984, pp. 76 etc.). In January 1852 his name was proposed for membership of the Brotherhood in place of Collinson, but before the election could be formally ratified 'the . . . Brotherhood', in William Rossetti's words, 'tho' never expressly dissolved or discontinued, had ceased to have any corporate solidity, and so the question of Deverell's election was no further raised'. The name of Millais's disciple Charles Allston Collins, whose promising career petered out in morbid self-distrust, had also recently been proposed but met with opposition. Another member of the circle was the painter of *April Love*, Arthur Hughes, but his first Pre-Raphaelite painting was not exhibited until 1852. All these artists subscribed to the original ideals of the PRB, which in the 1850s were seen as the way forward. Henry Holiday, a student at the Royal Academy Schools 1852–7, 'was proud to describe himself as a Pre-Raphaelite'. But the fragile unity of the Brotherhood itself soon disintegrated and Hunt, Rossetti and Millais went their separate ways. Hunt remained faithful to Pre-Raphaelite ideals as he interpreted them, but Millais' early inspiration faded, and after 1856, when he exhibited two masterpieces, *Autumn Leaves* and *The Blind Girl*, his choice of subjects became increasingly insipid.

Rossetti, on the other hand, began his first 'Froissartian' watercolour, *Arthur's Tomb* (no. 10), in 1854, and in this romantic mediaevalism he found his true vein. What might be called the 'second wave' of Pre-Raphaelitism which sprang from it dates from 1856, when Edward Burne Jones and William Morris made Rossetti's acquaintance and Burne Jones became his pupil. The quality of Burne Jones's art is summed up in his definition of a picture as 'a beautiful romantic dream of something that never was, never will be . . . in a land no one can define or remember, only desire'. A convincing parallel has even been drawn between him and the contemporary French Symbolist Gustave Moreau. Nothing could be further from Holman Hunt; but in the literal sense of the word, Burne Jones, with his undisguised homage to Botticelli and Mantegna, can also be called a Pre-Raphaelite. Morris, after a brief experiment with painting, found that the right direction for his genius lay in the decorative arts. His particular contribution to the Pre-Raphaelite Movement and to late nineteenth-century taste was the involvement of Rossetti, Madox Brown, Burne Jones and others in the activities of 'The Firm' which he founded in 1861.

In 1854 Rossetti wrote to William Bell Scott about a project for 'a Sketching Club, to be called the *Folio* . . . a folio is to be sent round to all the members in rotation, each one to put in a drawing whenever it reaches him, taking out his former one. Eighteen members have been named conjecturally'. Though there are occasional references to the *Folio* in later letters, the project never got off the ground; but that it should even have been proposed emphasises the importance of the drawing as an essential element in Pre-Raphaelite art. Raphael – to cite the obvious antithesis – made many drawings, of the greatest beauty, but always as preparatory studies, the end-product being invariably a painting. The utilitarian view of the purpose of drawing was largely shared by Holman Hunt and Madox Brown, and it must be admitted that their drawings are the least interesting part of their work. But for Rossetti and Millais drawing provided a means of expression complete in itself. Rossetti disliked the drudgery of oil painting, and for the greater part of the 1850s abandoned it, except for the never completed and perpetually vexatious '*Found*' (see no. 8). Some finished compositions (e.g. the study for '*Found*', and *Hamlet and Ophelia*, nos. 8 and 23) are highly wrought in pen and ink, while for others (e.g. *Arthur's Tomb*) he used his own individual technique of watercolour painting. Equally, some of Millais's most beautiful early works are finished drawings, ranging from *The Eve of the Deluge* of about 1850 (no. 39) to the 'Modern Life' subjects of 1853–4 (nos. 43 and 44). The notion of a drawing as a work complete in itself was encouraged by the revival of book-illustration in the 1850s brought about by the perfecting of wood-engraving as a means of reproduction.

The Pre-Raphaelites derived their knowledge of early art mainly from engravings, especially those by Dürer. The angular folds of the drapery in Rossetti's drawing of *The Sleeper*, dateable 1848–9 (no. 6), reflect this influence; and Burne Jones, though a later arrival in the Pre-Raphaelite circle, adopted the same engraver-like technique for his early pen and ink drawings made under the direct inspiration of Rossetti. Another source was the series of engravings by Giovanni Paolo Lasinio after the Giottesque frescoes in the Campo Santo at Pisa, published in 1832. However misleading as records of the original paintings, their wiry contours and areas of regular hatching are clearly echoed in Millais' early, highly detailed pen and ink style of drawing, as in the elaborate composition *The Disentombment of Queen Matilda* of 1849 (Tate Gallery: cf. Arts Council Exh. 1979, p. 9). The deliberate regular action of the engraving tool on the plate does not admit of any variation of emphasis in the line, and when translated into drawing can sometimes verge on the diagrammatic, as in Holman Hunt's composition study for his *Valentine and Proteus* of 1851 (no. 1).

The British Museum's collection of Pre-Raphaelite drawings, though small by comparison with that in the Birmingham City Art Gallery, includes some of the first importance. It would be satisfactory to be able to record that the Museum authorities in the 1850s were quick to take advantage of this sudden flowering of native genius, but as often happens, only after the lapse of a generation was it appreciated; it was not until 1885 that the Museum acquired its first Pre-Raphaelite drawing (no. 17). The collection has not been systematically built up, but is the result of casual purchasing as opportunity arose (some outstanding drawings have been added in recent years), and two notable bequests, those of Colonel William Gillum in 1910 and of Cecil French in 1954. An interesting feature is the group of eighteen drawings by Charles Allston Collins, bought in 1891 from the great Pre-Raphaelite collector Charles Fairfax Murray, the bulk of whose collection was to pass to Birmingham only thirteen years later.

This exhibition is an anthology, and an anthologist has some right to pick and choose. Not every drawing in the collection that can be described as 'Pre-Raphaelite' is included, but an appendix to the catalogue provides a list of all drawings by the artists represented. The catalogue itself begins with the members of the Brotherhood – Holman Hunt, Rossetti and Millais, plus one (wholly un-Pre-Raphaelite) drawing by Thomas Woolner. The other artists are listed alphabetically. The exhibition does not follow this order, but is arranged as far as possible chronologically except for the section devoted to Pre-Raphaelite Landscape. On the whole 'the tame delineation of a given spot' did not greatly interest the Brotherhood, for whom landscape was a setting for a human drama. Millais's disciple Charles Collins seems to have been the first to apply to 'pure' landscape the principle of absolute truth to nature, in his *May in the Regent's Park* of 1851 (Tate: Pre-Raphaelite Exh. 1984, no. 43), of which a contemporary critic complained 'the botanical predominates altogether over the artistical'. Hunt's *Strayed Sheep* of 1852 (Tate: Pre-Raphaelite Exh. 1984, no. 48), which seems at first sight to be only a landscape, was intended as a political-cum-religious allegory; but simultaneously he was painting the small-scale *Fairlight Downs – Sunlight on the Sea* (private collection: Tate Pre-Raphaelite Exh. 1984, no. 52), similar in spirit to some of Madox Brown's small-scale landscapes of the 1850s. Of the watercolour landscape drawings here exhibited, the most truly Pre-Raphaelite are the *Scottish Farmstead* by Millais's brother William (no. 101) which may also be as early as 1853–4, and the 'close-up' of pansies and fern-shoots by John Brett (no. 52). A later development of landscape with its roots in Pre-Raphaelitism, is the work of the 'Idyllists', J. W. North and Fred Walker (nos. 103 and 117).

The group includes a watercolour by John Ruskin. He is sometimes thought of as one of the originators of the movement, but though some of the opinions in *Modern Painters* (1843) anticipate the Pre-Raphaelite creed, they were independent expressions of the *Zeitgeist*. Ruskin played an important part in the history of the movement, as its champion in the face of academic opposition and as the enlightened and generous patron who enabled Rossetti to continue painting the watercolours which are now considered his best work.

The group of comic drawings by Rossetti (nos. 25–32) and Burne Jones (nos. 63–69), mostly making fun of Morris, reveal a robust humour impossible to imagine from their other work.

Acknowledgements

I have to thank Antony Griffiths, Keeper of Prints and Drawings, for inviting me to select and catalogue this exhibition, and Kim Sloan for her invaluable help in editing the manuscript and reducing it to order. Acknowledgment is also due to her predecessor in charge of the British section of the collection, Lindsay Stainton, who was responsible for adding to the collection a number of drawings of the first importance (e.g. nos. 9, 10 and 11 by Rossetti, and 43 and 44 by Millais). Virginia Surtees and John Christian patiently answered my questions respectively about Rossetti and Burne Jones. My greatest debt is to my wife for her unfailing encouragement and practical advice.

J. A. GERE

List of Artists

The Catalogue

William Holman Hunt

(1827–1910)

Holman Hunt came to know Rossetti and Millais at the Royal Academy Schools, and in 1848 joined them in founding the Pre-Raphaelite Brotherhood. His earliest subjects were either historical, like *Rienzi* (1849) or *A Converted British Family sheltering a Christian Priest from the Persecution of the Druids* (1850), or taken from Keats and Shakespeare, like *Madeleine and Porphyro* (1848), *Claudio and Isabella* (1850) and *Valentine and Sylvia* (1851). In 1853 he exhibited two landscapes, *The Hireling Shepherd* and *Our English Coasts, 1852 (Strayed Sheep)*, each conveying an implicit rather than an overt moral; and in 1854 *The Light of the World* and his first 'modern' moralising subject *The Awakening Conscience*. In the same year he went to Palestine, in accordance with the doctrine of 'Truth to Nature' to paint biblical subjects in their authentic settings. *The Scapegoat* (exhibited 1856) is the best-known result of this expedition. He paid two further visits to Palestine, in 1869 and 1875.

All his life Holman Hunt remained faithful to the doctrines of Pre-Raphaelitism, as he understood them and as he expounded them in his autobiographical *Pre-Raphaelitism and the Pre-Raphaelite Brotherhood* (1905). His later paintings are no less carefully detailed, but they seem somehow overweighted by their own elaboration.

1 Valentine rescuing Silvia from Proteus

Pen and black ink, with some traces of underdrawing, and the head of the kneeling figure (Silvia) wholly in pencil.
237 × 321 mm (image, arched top), 267 × 366 mm (sheet)

Inscribed lower l., in pencil: *W. Holman Hunt. The Two Gentlemen of Verona*

1927–3–12–1 Presented by Mrs Holman Hunt, the artist's widow

Literature: Holman Hunt Exh., Liverpool 1969, no. 116, repr.; Tate Exh., 1984, no. 36

A study for the painting dated 1851 (Birmingham). The subject is taken from the last scene of Shakespeare's comedy *Two Gentlemen of Verona*. Valentine, one of the Two Gentlemen, has been banished from Milan for presuming to pay court to the Duke's daughter Silvia. His friend Proteus, the other Gentleman, takes advantage of his absence to woo her, and employs as go-between his own betrothed Julia, who has disguised herself as a boy and is thus, by dramatic convention, unrecognisable. Silvia goes in search of Valentine, who has joined a band of outlaws. She is followed by Proteus, and he by Julia, still in her disguise. The party is captured by the outlaws, and Valentine overhears Proteus threatening to ravish Silvia. He intervenes, but forgives him, and the play ends with a general reconciliation. In the drawing Valentine's gesture repels Proteus, but in the painting he clasps his hand in token of forgiveness; less significant differences are in the pose of Silvia and Julia's more elaborate costume.

Hunt does not explain why he chose this particular subject from one of Shakespeare's less well-known plays. He found it necessary to have inscribed on the frame a passage from the dialogue between Valentine and Proteus, but even so the complex relationship between the four characters is by no means obvious.

1

2 'The Lady of Shalott'
Verso: Study of a figure

Pen and brown ink, on very thin paper.
186 × 247 mm (irregular)

Provenance: the artist's granddaughter, Mrs Elizabeth Burt; her sale, Sotheby's, 10 October 1985, lot 37, purchased by the Museum

1985–11–9–15

Literature: Holman Hunt Exh., Liverpool 1969, no. 184

A sketch for an unexecuted illustration to *The Lady of Shalott* in the edition of Tennyson's poems published in 1857 by Edward Moxon. The publisher employed a variety of illustrators, incongruously associating Rossetti, Millais and Holman Hunt with such minor Academicians as Horsley, Clarkson Stanfield, Maclise and Creswick. Nevertheless, with its five illustrations by Rossetti, seven by Hunt and eighteen by Millais, Moxon's *Tennyson* is one of the most notable illustrated books of the period; and if he had had the discriminating taste to do as Rossetti thought he should have done, it would unquestionably have been the most beautiful. 'The right names', Rossetti wrote to William Allingham on 23 January 1855, 'would have been Millais, Hunt, Madox Brown, Hughes, a certain lady [i.e. Elizabeth Siddal] and myself. NO OTHERS'.

In the same letter Rossetti goes on to expound his theory of illustration: 'I fancy I shall try the *Vision of Sin* and *Palace of Art*, etc., – those where one can allegorize on one's own hook on the subject of the poem, without killing, for oneself and everyone, a distinct idea of the poet's. This, I fancy, is *always* the upshot of illustrated editions . . . unless where the poetry is so absolutely narrative as in the old ballads, for instance. Are we to try the experiment ever in their regard?

There are one or two or more of Tennyson's in narrative – but generally the worst, I think – *Lady Clare (sic)*, *Lord of Burleigh*, to wit'.

Mysterious though its story is, *The Lady of Shalott* must have had enough narrative character to appeal to him, for he persuaded Hunt, who had undertaken to provide two drawings for it, to let him do the second one, illustrating the end of the poem in which the Lady, having looked out of the window in defiance of the curse laid on her, floats down the river to Camelot in a boat, and then dies. Rossetti's illustration differs from Hunt's sketch in showing the boat after its arrival at Camelot, with Sir Lancelot, for whose sake she had disregarded the curse, gazing down at the dead Lady in the boat.

The illustration to *The Lady of Shalott* that Hunt did reserve for himself was to the lines

Out flew the web and floated wide
The mirror cracked from side to side.

He later used the composition for a painting now in the Manchester Art Gallery (Holman Hunt Exh., Liverpool 1969, no. 78), a larger version of which is in the Wadsworth Atheneum at Hartford, Connecticut. It was developed from an earlier drawing, made probably in 1850 (1969 Exh., no. 119, pl. 31).

Thirteen sketches by Hunt for illustrations to the Moxon *Tennyson* were in the 1969 Exh. (nos. 180–192). He himself reproduced eight in *Pre-Raphaelitism* (1905, ii. pp. 98–103 and 107), and two more in the second edition (1913, ii, pp. 70–76 and 79). His headpiece for the poem *Recollections of the Arabian Nights*, of a man in oriental dress reclining in a boat, may be an adaptation of another solution for the *Lady of Shalott* illustration.

2

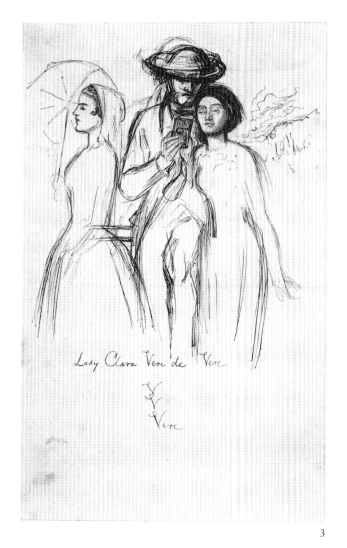

3

4

3 'Lady Clara Vere de Vere'

Pen and brown ink. 180 × 114 mm

Inscribed with title as above, followed by *V/V/Vere*

Provenance: Charles Pollitt ('friend and pupil of the artist');
purchased from Julian Hartnoll

1992–4–4–23

Nos. 3 and 4 are sketches for a never-executed illustration in
Moxon's edition of Tennyson's poems (see no. 2). The poem
Lady Clara Vere de Vere, perhaps best remembered for the
sentiment 'Kind hearts are more than coronets, And simple
faith than Norman blood', consists of a denunciation of
Lady Clara, a heartless aristocratic beauty who 'thought to
break a country heart For pastime, ere you went to town'

and drove her humble admirer to suicide. Besides being one of Tennyson's unhappiest efforts, the poem does not lend itself to effective illustration and it is not surprising that Hunt abandoned the idea.

In the drawing, a lady with a parasol seems to be walking haughtily past Lady Clara and her admirer; but there is no such third person in the poem, and one can only suppose that she is not part of the group but an alternative idea for Lady Clara – a supposition supported by her supercilious expression.

4 A Man embracing a Woman

Verso: Sketch of a Man

Pen and brown ink. 180 × 114 mm

Provenance: as for no. 3

1992–4–4–24

Like no. 3, a sketch for an illustration to Tennyson's poem *Lady Clara Vere de Vere*. The two sheets are said originally to have been halves of a folded sheet of note-paper. One of them is blind-stamped 'Extra Super Ivory'.

5 A Man in Eastern Costume, walking to the right with a Basket on his Back

Metalpoint on a white prepared ground. 478 × 296 mm

Signed near lower edge with monogram, and dated *1876*

1927–3–12–2 Presented by Mrs Holman Hunt

Literature: Hunt, *Pre-Raphaelitism*, ii, p. 323; Bennett, Merseyside Colls. Cat., 1988, p. 89

A study for the figure of St Joseph, carrying his carpenter's tools on his back and leading the donkey bearing the Virgin and the Infant Christ, in *The Triumph of the Innocents* (Walker Art Gallery, Liverpool). The subject is essentially the *Flight into Egypt*, escorted by the souls of the Innocents massacred by King Herod. The painting was begun in Jerusalem, on Hunt's third visit to Palestine in 1875–8.

5

Dante Gabriel Rossetti
(1828–1882)

Rossetti's father, Gabriele Rossetti, a political exile from the Kingdom of Naples, had settled in London where he became Professor of Italian, well known as a learned commentator on Dante; his mother's brother Dr John Polidori (d. 1821), was briefly Byron's travelling physician, and author of the supernatural story *The Vampyre* sometimes mistakenly attributed to his employer; Christina Rossetti, the poet, was a sister. Brought up in this literary atmosphere, Dante Gabriel Rossetti found it hard to decide whether to devote himself to poetry or to painting. Though, as things turned out, he distinguished himself equally in both, initially he chose to be a painter; but his impatience with the drudgery of artistic training prevented him from acquiring the technical mastery of his fellow-students Holman Hunt and Millais, with whom in 1848 he founded the Pre-Raphaelite Brotherhood.

Only his very earliest paintings, *The Girlhood of Mary Virgin* (1848–9) and *Ecce Ancilla Domini* (1849–50), can be called Pre-Raphaelite in the strict technical sense. His one attempt at a 'modern moral' subject, *Found*, which he began in 1854, was a fiasco (see no. 8). All these were in oil, but in the 1850s he preferred to express himself in drawings and in watercolour, in which he developed an individual technique. His watercolours are best described as small-scale paintings, in which minutely hatched, diapered and stippled layers of intense colour, strengthened by the addition of bodycolour or gum, are applied with an almost dry brush. They are characterised by a vague poetic mediaevalism and romantic archaism, with none of the respect for historical accuracy that marks the orthodox Pre-Raphaelite treatment of subjects from history and literature.

'These chivalrous, Froissartian themes', he wrote, 'are quite a passion of mine.' The passion was shared by his younger friends William Morris and Edward Burne Jones, whose admiration and enthusiasm for a time provided the stimulus he needed when the first flush of romantic excitement was beginning to fade. But the small oil-painting *Bocca Baciata*, painted in 1859, is the first of the long series of half- or three-quarter-length figures of languid women which dominate his work from the mid-1860s. As often happens with English romantic artists, Rossetti's creative and imaginative powers began to wane before he was forty, and in his case the decline was accelerated by neurasthenia, insomnia, dependence on drugs and a form of persecution mania, aggravated by Robert Buchanan's attack in 1871 on 'The Fleshly School of Poetry' (see no. 19), which cut him off from most of his friends and turned him into a recluse.

6 'The Sleeper'

Pen and black ink, surrounded by border of pink bodycolour, strips at top and centre of lower edge added. 223 × 118mm (image), 265 × 173mm (sheet)

Inscribed in ink, top l.: *E. A. POE*; top r.: *D. G. ROSSETTI*; below: *The Sleeper*

Provenance: given by Rossetti to the painter Lowes Cato Dickinson; his son, Goldsworthy Lowes Dickinson; his sister; Messrs Watford, Wilson & Co., from whom purchased by Museum, through H. L. Florence Fund

1936–6–8–1

Literature: S 29

The poem of this name by Edgar Allen Poe is too long to quote in full; the passage illustrated is:

I pray to God that she may lie
Forever with unopened eye,
While the pale sheeted ghosts go by.

Some of Rossetti's early drawings in the manner of lithographs by Devéria and Delacroix are dated as late as 1848. *The Sleeper* and other illustrations to Poe's poems (e.g. *The Raven* and *Ulalame*, S 10A, 19B and 30), though still somewhat hesitant in handling, show the beginning of the development of a distinctively Pre-Raphaelite style of drawing and can hardly be any earlier. The scratchy penwork and angular drapery in *The Sleeper* suggest the influence of German fifteenth-century engravings.

The Sleeper.

6

7 Head of a Girl

Black chalk and grey wash over pencil. 166 × 126 mm

Provenance: Rossetti Sale, Christie's, 12 May 1883, lot 207; Colonel Gillum, by whom bequeathed

1910–12–10–7

Literature: S 544

The style indicates an early date, perhaps as early as 1849, as Virginia Surtees suggests. She pointed out the resemblance between this head and one reproduced by Marillier (p. 34) and described as a fragment, then in the possession of W. M. Rossetti, of the original unfinished large-scale painting *'Hist!' said Kate the Queen* (a subject taken from a song in Browning's poem *Pippa Passes*), begun in 1849 and later destroyed. The composition is known in its complete form from a smaller version, dated 1851, belonging to Eton College (S 49; Tate Exh., 1984, no. 31). The drawing is not a study for the head in the fragment, which must be that of the attendant standing immediately to the left of the queen, but could well be from the same model.

8 Found

Pen and brown wash, heightened with white on the woman's skirt, face and hair. Some touches of pen and black ink on the calf in the cart. 205 × 182 mm

Signed with monogram and dated 1853. Inscribed along lower edge: *I remember thee: the kindness of thy youth, the love of thy betrothal* (Jeremiah 2: 2, with 'espousals' altered to 'betrothal'); and on the gravestone visible through the railings top l.: *There is m[ore] joy am[ong]/ the ange[l]s in hea[ven]/ one sinn[e]r that . . .* (cf. Luke 15: 7)

Provenance: Colonel Gillum, (according to a note in the departmental register of acquisitions, presumably transcribed from the old frame, bought from the artist in 1860), by whom bequeathed

1910–12–10–1

Literature: M 35(1); S 64B; Grieve 1978, p. 2; Tate Exh., 1984, no. 186

Found was Rossetti's only attempt at painting a 'modern moral' subject according to strict Pre-Raphaelite principles of truth to nature. He described his intention in a letter to Holman Hunt, dated 30 January 1855 (see under S 64): 'The subject had been sometime designed before you left England and will be thought by anyone who sees it when (and if) finished, to follow in the wake of your "Awakened Conscience", but not by yourself, as you know I had long had in view subjects taking the same direction as my present one. The picture represents a London street at dawn, with the lamps still lighted along a bridge which forms the distant background. A drover has left his cart standing in the middle of the road (in which, *i.e.* the cart, stands baa-ing a calf on its way to market), and has run a little way after a girl who has passed him, wandering in the streets. He has just come up with her, and she, recognising him, has sunk under her shame upon her knees, against the wall of a raised churchyard in the foreground, while he stands holding her hands as he seized them, half in bewilderment and half guarding her from doing herself a hurt . . . The calf, a white one, will be a beautiful and suggestive part of the thing, though I am far from having painted him as well as I hoped to do – perhaps through my having performed the feat, necessarily an open-air one, in the time just preceding Christmas, and also through the great difficulty of the net drawn over him; the motion constantly throwing one out – me especially, quite new as I was to any animal painting'.

Hunt's *Awakening Conscience* (Tate Gallery), exhibited at the Royal Academy in the previous year, also treated the theme of the repentant 'fallen woman', as did Rossetti in the drawing *Hesterna Rosa* of 1853 (S 57; Tate Gallery) and the somewhat later watercolour of 1857, *The Gate of Memory* (S 100; private collection). Millais did not attempt a painting of it, but some of his 1853–4 drawings of contemporary subjects (see nos. 43 and 44) treat 'unconsecrated passion in modern life'. Interest in the theme extended to the outermost fringe of the Pre-Raphaelite circle. A drawing entitled *The Castaways*, contributed by Anna Maria Howitt to the Pre-Raphaelite circulating sketching club, The Folio, was described by Rossetti as 'a rather strong-minded subject, involving a dejected female, mud with lilies lying in it, a dust-heap and other details; and symbolic of something improper . . . of course, seriously, Miss H. is quite right in painting it, if she chooses, and she is

7

doing so. I daresay it will be a good picture' (Letter to W. Allingham, August 1854).

The cautious reservation 'when (and if) finished' in Rossetti's letter to Hunt was prophetic. He found the subject uncongenial – as his fellow Pre-Raphaelite Brother F. G. Stephens said, he 'was thoroughly indisposed towards attempts to ameliorate anybody's condition by means of pictures' – and the laborious technique increasingly wearisome. 'Gabriel getting on slowly with his calf' recorded Madox Brown impatiently in his journal in November 1854 'he paints it in all like Albert Durer hair by hair & seems incapable of any breadth. . . . From want of habit I see nature bothers him – but it is sweetly drawn and felt'. *Found* was to be a source of continual vexation for the rest of Rossetti's life. More than one of his faithful patrons commissioned him to complete it, but he could never bring himself to do so, and was still working on it as late as 1880. The unfinished canvas was tidied up by his studio-assistant H. Treffry Dunn and by Burne Jones, and is now in the Wilmington Society of Fine Arts (Bancroft Collection), Delaware, USA. Its appearance as Rossetti left it is illustrated by Marillier opposite p. 44.

9 Hamlet and Ophelia

Pen and brown wash, over pencil. 258 × 181 mm

Inscribed in ink by Rossetti: *Hamlet & Ophelia* and in pencil very faintly in lower r. corner: *D. G. Rossetti to* [the name of the recipient is difficult to read, but it could be *S. Solomon*]

Provenance: Simeon Solomon ? (see above); Henry Holiday (according to label on back of old frame. He and Solomon had been fellow-students at the Royal Academy Schools in the 1850s and close friends); anonymous sale, Bath, Messrs Jolly, 4 March 1974, lot 175, bought Agnew for the Museum

1974–4–6–11

Literature: J. A. Gere, *British Museum Yearbook*, i (1976), pp. 277 ff.

This simpler, and evidently earlier, treatment of the subject of no. 23 (q.v.) did not come to light until after the publica-

tion of Virginia Surtees's catalogue. It can hardly be much later than *c.*1854. Another drawing of the two figures, in Birmingham (S 108A), could be even earlier.

10 Arthur's Tomb

COLOUR PLATE I

Watercolour. 233 × 374 mm (image), 241 × 382 mm (sheet)

Signed with monogram and inscribed *Arthur's Tomb 1854*

Provenance: commissioned in 1855 by John Ruskin; George Butterworth; bought back by Rossetti in 1878; William Graham (sale, Christie's, 3 April 1886, lot 102); S. Pepys Cockerell; by descent to his grandson, E. W. Huddart (sale, Christie's, 4 June 1982, lot 24); bought by Museum

1982–6–19–23

Literature: M 38; S 73; Evelyn Waugh, *Rossetti: His Life and Works* (1928), pp. 93–5; Rossetti Exh., RA 1973, no. 132; Tate Exh., 1984, no. 213, repr.

Virginia Surtees points out that Rossetti must have inscribed the date 1854 from memory, and that his memory deceived him: in a letter dated 17 September 1855 he tells Madox Brown 'That drawing of *Launcelot* is all but finished'.

In the same month, in a bookshop in Birmingham, William Morris and Edward Burne Jones, then still undergraduates at Oxford, came across Southey's 1827 edition of Sir Thomas Malory's late-fifteenth-century narrative of the legendary history of King Arthur and the Knights of the Round Table. *The Morte d'Arthur* was exactly in tune with their particular taste for romantic mediaevalism, and when they met Rossetti for the first time a few months later they were encouraged to find that he shared their enthusiasm to the point of declaring that *The Morte d'Arthur* and the Bible were 'the two greatest books in the world'. *Arthur's Tomb*, the first and arguably the finest of Rossetti's 'Arthurian' subjects, dates from before that first meeting (his interest in the theme was no doubt inspired by Dante's reference to Lancelot in the Paolo and Francesca passage of which he was making drawings as early as 1849: see no. 11); but it was the combination of his enthusiasm and that of his two younger disciples that resulted in the decoration of the hall of the Oxford Union in the summer of 1857 (see no. 17).

8

Hamlet & Ophelia

In the admirable analysis of the composition in his life of Rossetti (1928) Evelyn Waugh showed that he departed dramatically from Malory's account, in which the widowed Queen Guenevere, attended by the ladies and gentlemen of her court, takes an 'affecting and decorous' farewell of her lover Sir Launcelot in the cloister of the convent to which she had retired after King Arthur's death. In the watercolour 'The lovers meet alone and at Arthur's tomb, and the dead king's effigy dominates the composition. Austere and ungainly, it draws a line of obtrusive mortality across the picture. On one side is Launcelot, all the sentimental despondence of Malory aflame with masculinity, crouching and peering under the beetle-back of his shield like some obscene and predatory insect; the head of Arthur butts him away with almost comic vigour. Beside the tomb, and practically a part of it, kneels Guinever, stripped of the sententious dignity of the abbess-queen, her stiff gesture of repugnance allying her with the archaic sculpture at her back, the last defence of threatened chastity, Galatea repetrified. It is in many ways a painful picture. Three horizontals constrict the composition until it aches with suppressed resilience. Remove the apple-tree and the whole composition would fly up uncontrollably through the frame; the thick, stiff little trunk straps it down and tortures it unendurably . . . A lesser artist, certainly any other Pre-Raphaelite, would have twisted that apple-tree or gnarled it and made a beautiful decoration of it; all Rossetti wanted was a clamp'.

Arthur's Tomb was not to Ruskin's taste, and before long he gave it away to one of his pupils at the Working Men's College, George Butterworth. Soon after receiving it from Rossetti, he wrote to his friend Ellen Heaton: 'The Guinevere and Launcelot is not my pet drawing, though Mr Browning could not say too much of it – it is one of my imperfect ones – the Launcelot is so funnily bent under his shield, and Arthur points his toes so over the tomb, that I dare not show it to Anti-Pre-Raphaelites, but I value it intensely myself'. The reference to Robert Browning's admiration is significant, for this drawing is the pictorial equivalent of one of his *Dramatic Lyrics* describing intensely charged moments of emotional crisis. Morris's own poem 'King Arthur's Tomb' in his early volume, *The Defence of Guenevere* (1858) is inspired by the drawing; and when asked in whose style another poem in the volume was written, he is said to have answered 'More like Browning than any one else, I suppose'.

11 Paolo and Francesca

Pencil. 225 × 167 mm

Inscribed in pencil along lower edge: *Dante G. Rossetti to his friend Alex. Munro*

Provenance: Alexander Munro; thence by descent until sale, Christie's, 16 October 1981, lot 16; bought in and later purchased by the Museum

1981–11–7–17

Literature: M under no. 41; Ironside & Gere, pl. 32; S 75A; Rossetti Exh., RA 1973, no. 99

The drawing is a study for the left-hand compartment of the tripartite watercolour in the Tate Gallery (S 75), the differences being in the position of Paolo's legs and that there the book is larger and resting securely on his and Francesca's knees. On the watercolour are inscribed the lines from the passage in Canto 5 of the *Inferno* in which Dante describes his encounter with the guilty lovers Paolo and Francesca da Rimini:

> . . . O lasso,
> quanti dolci pensier, quanto disio
> meno costoro al doloroso passo!

Rossetti had 'been brought up on' Dante, after whom he was named and on whom his father, Gabriele Rossetti, had written a learned commentary. This well-known passage, one of the most sensuous, and most beautiful, in the *Divina Commedia*, clearly made a particular appeal to him.

The right-hand compartment of the watercolour shows the lovers floating in the flames of hell-fire, and the narrower one in the centre, the figures of Dante and Virgil. It is not dated, but Rossetti is recorded as having painted it in a week in October or November 1855 after hearing that Miss Siddal was stranded penniless in Paris. He sold the drawing to Ruskin for 35 guineas and hurried to Paris with the money.

Rossetti had long been thinking of treating the subject in this way, for in *The Pre-Raphaelite Journal* on 19 November

Dante G. Rossetti to his friend Alex. Munro.

28

1849 W. M. Rossetti recorded that 'Gabriel . . . intends that the picture shall be in three compartments. In the middle, Paolo and Francesca kissing, on the left Dante and Virgil in the second circle; on the right the spirits blowing to and fro'.

It is significant that Munro should have owned three other drawings by Rossetti of the embrace of Paolo and Francesca (S 75B, C and E), one of which is in the pre-Pre-Raphaelite style of about 1846–8 inspired by the *Faust* lithographs of Delacroix. A sheet of four sketches in pen and wash had belonged to W. M. Rossetti and is now in the collection of Mr John Baskett (S 75D). In the Great Exhibition of 1851 Munro exhibited a plaster model of the group which attracted the attention of Mr Gladstone, a life-long lover of Dante. He commissioned the half-life-size version in marble, signed and dated 1852, which the Birmingham Art Gallery acquired in 1963 (see *Burlington Magazine*, cv (1963), p. 509). Comparison with Rossetti's drawings (especially the central sketch on S 75D) leaves no doubt that this was the source of Munro's composition.

Munro gave a cast of the model to Rossetti, who refers to it in a letter of 8 January 1853 to Madox Brown; it was lot 223 in the sale of the contents of no. 16 Cheyne Walk on 5 July 1882.

12 Miss Siddal standing

Pen and brown wash. 135 × 52 mm

Provenance: Campbell Dodgson, by whom presented

1912–11–9–5

Literature: S 497

The figure's upright stance and downward glance suggested to Virginia Surtees that Rossetti may have made this sketch when designing the illustration of the three spinning 'Maids of Elfen-Mere' for William Allingham's *The Music Master* (1855).

12

13

13 Miss Siddal in a Basket Chair

Pencil. 188 × 153 mm

Provenance: G. Bellingham-Smith; R.E.A. Wilson; bought from him in 1932 by Cecil French, by whom bequeathed

1954–5–8–3

Literature: S 498

14 Miss Siddal in a Basket Chair

Pencil. 177 × 185 mm

Provenance: Rossetti Sale, Christie's, 12 May 1883, lot 121; Colonel Gillum, by whom bequeathed

1910–12–10–6

Literature: S 496

See no. 15.

15 Miss Siddal in an Armchair

Pencil. 184 × 118 mm

Provenance: Rossetti Sale, Christie's, 12 May 1883, lot 121;
Colonel Gillum, by whom bequeathed

1910–12–10–5

Literature: S 495

Rossetti, one of whose pet names for Elizabeth Siddal was
'Guggum' or 'Gug', never tired of drawing her. Madox
Brown's diary records in October 1854 'Gabriel as usual
diffuse and inconsequent in his work. Drawing wonderful
and lovely "Guggums" one after another, each one a fresh
charm, each one stamped with immortality, and his picture
[*Found*, see no. 8] never advancing'; and again in August
1855, 'He showed me a drawer full of "Guggums", God
knows how many, but not bad work I should say for the six
years he has known her. It is like a monomania with him.
Many of them are matchless in beauty however and one day
will be worth large sums'. No fewer than fifty-eight drawings of her were listed by Virginia Surtees, and a further six
have since come to light. Almost all were exhibited at the
Ashmolean Museum, Oxford, in 1991, with a fully illustrated catalogue by Mrs Surtees. The four in the British
Museum were nos. 10, 19, 43 and 44 in the exhibition.

For Elizabeth Siddal see p. 135.

16 La Belle Dame sans Merci

Brush drawing in grey wash over pencil and some pen and
brown ink. 332 × 432 mm

Illustrating the fifth stanza of the poem by Keats, inscribed in
pencil by Rossetti on the drawing: *I set her on my pacing steed/
And nothing else saw all day long/ For sideways would she lean
& sing/ A fairies' song.*

Provenance: Rossetti Sale, Christie's, 12 May 1883, lot 84;
Colonel Gillum, by whom bequeathed

1910–12–10–2

Literature: M under no. 40; S 76B

The unusual scale and technique suggest that this may have
been the beginning of a watercolour, which was never
carried further. It probably dates from the mid-1850s, as
Virginia Surtees suggests. Rossetti treated the subject in
another, and less immediately recognisable, way, with the
two figures walking side by side, in a pen and brown wash
drawing dated 1848 (S 32, repr. Marillier, opp. p. 17) and a
watercolour dated 1855 (S 76). See also no. 100.

17 How Sir Galahad, Sir Bors and Sir Percival received the Sanc Grael; but Sir Percival's Sister died by the Way

Pen and brown ink with some pencil. 249 × 351 mm

Inscribed with the names of the figures: DOM GALAHAD
DOM PERCIVAL DOM. BORS SOROR D. PERCIVAL.

Provenance: Rossetti sale, Christie's, 12 May 1883, lot 65,
bought Lawrie, £11–11–0; sale, Christie's, 18 May 1885,
bought £7–7–0

1885–6–13–81

Literature: M 72; LB 1; S 94

In the spring of 1857 Rossetti and William Morris visited
Oxford, where the architect Benjamin Woodward showed
them the Gothic-style building newly completed by him for
the Union Society. The upper part of the walls of the
Debating Hall (now the Old Library) was divided into bays
pierced by pairs of circular windows, and Woodward wel-
comed Rossetti's offer 'to paint figures of some kind' in one
of the spaces surrounding the windows, and Morris's offer
to decorate another (for Rossetti's account, see his letter of
June 1861 to Alexander Gilchrist).

At this point in Rossetti's career, when the original Pre-
Raphaelite Brotherhood had dissolved and his artistic aims
were diverging increasingly from those of Holman Hunt and
Millais, his circle of friends was enlarged by the addition of
Morris and Edward Burne Jones, who had now left Oxford
and come to live in London. To these younger men – in 1857
he was 29 and they 23 – he was an object of hero-worship,
whose pre-eminence they were fully prepared to acknow-
ledge; and it was they and four others, Arthur Hughes (q.v.),
Spencer Stanhope, Val Prinsep and John Hungerford Pollen,
who in the summer of 1857 undertook under his leadership
the decoration of the Oxford Union.

15

16

17

Morris and Jones shared Rossetti's enthusiasm for *The Morte d'Arthur* (see no. 10), and it was inevitable that this should have provided the scheme of the decoration. The two subjects chosen by Rossetti were episodes in the Quest for the Holy Grail, one of the main themes of the Arthurian legend (the Grail was the cup or dish used at the Last Supper, said to have been preserved by St Joseph of Arimathea and taken by him to Glastonbury). Rossetti completed *Sir Lancelot's Vision of the Sanc Grael*, but *The Attainment of the Sanc Grael*, for which the present drawing is a study, was never begun. In 1864 he painted a watercolour of it (see no. 22).

The Union paintings are often described, incorrectly, as frescoes. A fresco is painted on freshly applied plaster while it is still damp, so that the pigment sinks into it and becomes permanent. Rossetti and his friends painted on nothing more substantial than the coat of whitewash covering the unplastered brick wall. (It is curious, but characteristic, that they should have known nothing of the experiments in the technique of fresco-painting made in the 1840s and '50s in connexion with the decoration of the rebuilt Houses of Parliament.) Their paintings rapidly deteriorated, and in spite of attempts to restore them are now almost indecipherable; but the large-scale watercolour study for *Lancelot's Vision* (Ashmolean Museum, Oxford; S 93A) shows that Coventry Patmore was not exaggerating when he described them as 'sweet, bright and pure as a cloud in the sunrise . . . so brilliant as to make the walls look like the margin of an illuminated manuscript'.

18 Mary Magdalene at the Door of Simon the Pharisee

Pen and brown ink with some wash. 66 × 61 mm

Provenance: Charles Augustus Howell (see document printed by Surtees); Campbell Dodgson, by whom presented 1912–11–9–4

Literature: M p. 96 footnote; S 109B

A first sketch for a composition of many figures, which reached its final form in a large, highly finished pen-and-ink drawing, dated 1858, in the Fitzwilliam Museum, Cambridge (S 109; Tate Exh., 1984, no. 223).

18

19 My Lady Greensleeves

Watercolour. 311 × 185 mm

Signed with monogram lower l., and inscribed top r. with four bars of music and the refrain of the ballad:
Greensleeves is my heart of gold
And who but my lady Greensleeves.
She is binding a sleeve round a helmet, as a 'favour'.

Provenance: George Rae (according to W. M. Rossetti, bought from the artist for £105); Revd E. Hale; Revd Stuart A. Donaldson (Master of Magdalene College, Cambridge); Cecil French, by whom bequeathed

1954–5–8–1

Literature: W. M. Rossetti, DGR as D & W, p. 42; M 67; S 113

W. M. Rossetti lists the drawing under the year 1859. In the late 1860s Rossetti's and Swinburne's poetry was the target of moralising disapproval, culminating in October 1871 in Thomas Buchanan's notorious attack on 'The Fleshly School of Poetry'. Rossetti's sensitivity to this adverse critical climate no doubt prompted the action earlier in the same year which he described in a letter to William Bell Scott (Letters, p. 964). Infuriated by an absurdly ill-informed criticism of this particular drawing in *Notes and Queries*, 'I sent to Agnews for the thing [and] gave it a good daubing all over, and transmogrified it so completely (title and all) as to separate it for ever, I hope, from this Bedlam correspondence'.

Rossetti's 'good daubing' seems to have been limited to the background, on which he must subsequently have re-inscribed the title. His friend and former studio-assistant Charles Fairfax Murray saw the drawing in Cambridge in about 1905, and is quoted by A. C. Benson (*Memories and Friends*, 1924, p. 218) as saying 'Rossetti spoilt that picture. It used to have a beautiful background of landscape, and a distant hill-town; but Rossetti, who was sore about some criticisms of his perspective, got it back from the possessor, and painted it all out'. In fact, the comments which upset Rossetti did not mention the background, or criticise the perspective.

W. M. Rossetti implies that George Rae had bought the drawing in 1863, and in 1889 names him as the owner; but by 1883 it was in the possession of Mr Hale, who lent it to an exhibition at the Burlington Fine Arts Club; and since there is no suggestion in Rossetti's letter that he asked the owner's permission to retouch the drawing, it seems likely that Rae sold it back to him before 1871, and that Rossetti himself had consigned it to Agnews for sale.

Two pencil studies for the figure, one with some watercolour, are in Birmingham (S 113A and B). In another treatment of the subject in oil, dated May 1863 (S 161; Fogg Museum, Harvard), the figure is shown half-length and full-face.

20 Writing on the Sand

Watercolour. 263 × 241 mm (begun on a smaller sheet of paper, enlarged on both sides and at the bottom by being stuck on a larger sheet to make room for the tip of the man's stick and the top of the head he is drawing, the toe of his shoe, and part of the lady's skirt and sleeve)

Signed lower r. with monogram and dated *1859*

Provenance: Ruth Herbert (see below); sale, Christie's, 25 May 1886, lot 120 (presumably her property: see S 335); Colnaghi, from whom purchased

1886–6–7–14

Literature: M, p. 219; LB 2; S 111; Tate Exh., 1984, no. 226; British Landscape Watercolours Exh., BM 1985, no. 191

Writing on the Sand is unique in Rossetti's work in treating a contemporary subject in light-hearted vein. The subject is a 'modern' one, but not in the spirit of *Found* and *The Gate of Memory* (see no. 8). Marillier, writing in the 1890s, found a drawing of 'men with Dundreary whiskers and women in hoops and Garibaldis quaint enough to be described as humorous'. He excluded it from the list of Rossetti's works at the end of his book, relegating it to a supplementary chapter on 'Early Drawings and Caricatures'. The features of the lady are unmistakeably those of Elizabeth Siddal, and Marillier states that the model for the man was (Sir) Richard Holmes (1835–1911), later Librarian at Windsor Castle.

In the very early days of the Pre-Raphaelite Brotherhood Rossetti was persuaded to paint a landscape according to strict Pre-Raphaelite principles of 'truthfulness to nature' to be used as background for some future picture, but the

19

20

experiment proved uncongenial and was not repeated. For the landscape setting of *Writing on the Sand* he took a short cut. His friend the landscape watercolourist George Pryce Boyce (see p. 78) recorded in his journal on 21 June 1858, 'Rossetti called and borrowed 2 sketches of mine on the coast of Babbacombe [near Torquay in S. Devon] as a help to background of a delicate little drawing of a loving couple on a sea beach on a windy day he is doing for Miss Herbert (rightly Mrs Crabbe) and would have me come down in a hansom to see the same'. For Miss Herbert see no. 105.

21 Cassandra

Pen and black ink. 330 × 464 mm

Signed with monogram lower r., and dated *1861*

Provenance: Colonel Gillum, by whom bequeathed

1910–12–10–4

Literature: M 110; S 127

A note in the departmental register of acquisitions, presumably copied from Gillum's inscription on the former frame, reads: *Drawn 1851–61, retouched 1867. Purchased directly from Rossetti.* The dating 1851–61 is difficult to explain: no drawing of this subject is referred to at that early date in Rossetti's published letters or in William Rossetti's conscientious *Dante Gabriel Rossetti as Designer and Writer* (1889), and in a letter of 1861, George Meredith, then one of Rossetti's circle of friends, tells his correspondent that 'Rossetti is going to illustrate my *Cassandra*, which *pome* has taken his heart' (*Letters of George Meredith*, 1912, i, p. 55). Had Rossetti already had the subject in mind ten years before (perhaps as a contribution to the circulating sketching club, The Folio), and if so, did he perhaps discuss his intention with Gillum? Nothing in the drawing itself suggests that it was begun in the early 1850s: its style is entirely consistent with the date 1861.

Cassandra, the daughter of King Priam, had the gift of prophecy and foretold the ruin of Troy in the Trojan War. Rossetti expounded the subject in a letter to Gillum quoted by Marillier (p. 108), who implies that its date is 1861: 'The incident is just before Hector's last battle. Cassandra has warned him in vain by her prophecies, and is now throwing herself against a pillar, and rending her clothes in despair, because he will not be detained longer. He is rushing down the steps and trying to make himself heard across her noise, as he shouts an order to the officer in charge of the soldiers who are going round the ramparts on their way to battle. One of his captains is beckoning to him to make haste. Behind him is Andromache with their child, and a nurse who is holding the cradle. Helen is arming Paris in a leisurely way on a sofa; we may presume from her expression that Cassandra has not spared her in her denunciations. Paris is patting her on the back to soothe her, much amused. Priam and Hecuba are behind, the latter stopping her ears in horror. One brother is imploring Cassandra to desist from her fear-inspiring cries. The ramparts are lined with engines for casting stones on the besiegers.'

22 How Sir Galahad, Sir Bors and Sir Percival received the Sanc Grael; but Sir Percival's Sister died by the Way

Pen and brown ink with some brown wash over pencil and some red chalk. The head, shoulders and upper right arm of Sir Galahad in pen and Indian ink. 251 × 351 mm

Provenance: Rossetti Sale, Christie's, 12 May 1883, lot 64; Colonel Gillum, by whom bequeathed

1910–12–10–3

Literature: M under 72; S 94A

So far as it goes, this drawing corresponds exactly with no. 17 except that the circular spaces for the windows, though indicated very faintly in red chalk, are disregarded, and the two rightmost figures hold their hands differently. They hold them in the same way in the watercolour of 1864 (Tate Gallery; S 94 R1), for which this drawing is probably a study. In handling it resembles no. 17, and it may be that Rossetti, who never carried out the projected mural of the composition, had the watercolour version in mind not long after the Union decoration came to a halt.

21

22

23 Hamlet and Ophelia

Pen and black ink, with touches of black wash.
308 × 261 mm

Signed with monogram, lower r. Inscriptions on strips of wood inserted in the under-mount, presumably from Gillum's frame, are on the same-coloured wood and in the same writing as that on *Cassandra*, another drawing in his bequest (no. 21). Two are passages from *Hamlet*, act III, scene i. The others are: *Thou shalt eat up thy leaves, and lose thy fruit, and leave thyself as a dry tree. Ecclesiasticus, chap.* VI [verse 3] and *Extol not thyself in the counsel of thine own heart, that thy soul be not torn in pieces:* [Ecclesiasticus 6: 2].

Provenance: Colonel Gillum, by whom bequeathed

1910–12–10–8

Literature: M 77; S 108; Tate Exh., 1984, no. 211

The scene in which Hamlet feigns madness in order to test Ophelia's constancy would have particularly appealed to Rossetti, whose most effective and dramatic compositions represent some highly charged moment of emotional tension or conflict between a man and a woman (as for example in *Found* and *Arthur's Tomb*, nos. 8 and 10). He had had the subject in mind as early as 1854, for in August of that year he wrote to William Allingham 'I don't know what design I shall put into the *Folio* [circulated by the Pre-Raphaelite sketching club]. I'm doing one of Hamlet and Ophelia which I meant for it – deeply symbolical and far-sighted, of course – but I fear I shall not get it done in time'.

Another drawing of the subject in the British Museum (no. 9) could be as early as 1854, and one in Birmingham (S 108A, pl. 153) even earlier; but these, like the later watercolour of 1866 (S 189), show little more than the two figures and can hardly have been described, even by their creator, as 'deeply symbolical and far-sighted' – words that imply that he was already thinking of something more elaborate on the lines of the Gillum drawing, as he described this in a letter of 23 April 1869 to Charles Eliot Norton: 'I mean [Hamlet] to be ramping about on the stalls of the little oratory turning out of the main hall, to which Ophelia has retired with the devotional book which her father gives her to read. He throws his arms wildly along the sill of the screen and frays the roses to pieces as he talks, hardly knowing what he says. She still holds out to him the letters and jewels which she wishes to return, but has done speaking and lets him rave on. In the woodwork are symbols of rash intro-spection – the Tree of Knowledge, and the man who touched the Ark and died. The outer court is full of intricate stairs and passages, and leads to the ramparts where the ghost walks at night'.

The Gillum drawing bears no date. Virginia Surtees follows Marillier in assigning it to 1858 and identifying it with one of the two pen and ink drawings, of *Hamlet* and *Guenevere*, which Rossetti's patron T. E. Plint bought from him at the beginning of 1859 for 40 guineas and 30 guineas respectively (letter to Madox Brown, 15 February). But on 28 September 1860 Rossetti asked for Brown's advice: 'I have nearly finished *Cassandra* pen-and-ink [see no. 21], at least with hard work might get it done within a day or two after the end of this month which is Gillum's quarter-day for my work [Gillum was evidently paying Rossetti a fixed annual sum in return for work supplied]. Now one of his commissions is for a £50 pen and ink (Hamlet). Do you not think I might propose a substitution of *Cassandra* for this, as ready for delivery (I remember he seemed taken with it)?'

Plint had died earlier in the year, but neither the *Hamlet* drawing nor the *Guenevere* were included in the sales of his collection at Christie's in March 1862 and June 1865. It has been suggested that Gillum acquired his *Hamlet* directly from Plint's executors, but this is not borne out by the wording of Rossetti's letter. Furthermore, a note in the departmental register of acquisitions, evidently transcribed from an inscription on the former frame or mount, states: *Executed for W. J. Gillum between Spring 1865 and May 1867. When we saw the Hamlet in 1865, the head of Hamlet only was drawn. Note by Col. Gillum.*

The combined evidence of Rossetti's letters and Gillum's note must lead to the conclusion that Gillum's *Hamlet* cannot be the drawing bought by Plint in 1859. Gillum's statement that when he and his wife saw the drawing in 1865 it had hardly been begun is surely conclusive. But if Plint's *Hamlet* was another drawing, also in pen and ink and (to judge from the price paid) no less elaborately finished, it is surprising that it has not reappeared; indeed, it is tempting to wonder whether it ever existed, and whether by 'bought'

23

Rossetti meant only that it had been commissioned and – all-important from his point of view – paid for in advance. The identification of the *Guenevere* with the large finished pen-and-ink drawing of *Lancelot in Guenevere's Chamber*, dated *Oxford 1857* and now in Birmingham (S 95) is equally an open question.

In the early 1860s his 'chronic shortage of tin' led Rossetti to demand payment in advance for commissions which he executed belatedly or sometimes not at all. At the beginning of 1866 he was still paying off his debt to Plint's executors; two years before, on 19 February 1864, he tells Madox Brown that he has written to Gillum 'with a proposal of delivering the pictures or refunding the money at dates fixed by agreement during the same time that I am paying off the Plint debt. He however prefers getting the pictures instead of the money and waiting to insure this until the Plint job is over. He was here today with his wife, very cordial and jolly, and so it stands'. The 'pictures' were presumably *Hamlet* and *Cassandra*, for they and the study for *Found* (bought in 1860, according to another note transcribed in the Register) are the only drawings in Gillum's bequest acquired directly from Rossetti himself; all the others came from the posthumous sale in 1883.

It may seem pedantic to dwell at such length on questions of provenance and dating, but this particular problem affects our view of Rossetti's artistic development. The drawing of *Hamlet and Ophelia* seems to fit stylistically with his work of the later 1850s rather than with that of the mid-1860s, and yet everything points to its having been begun in 1865 and completed in 1867.

24 Sheet of Grotesque Sketches

Pencil, on a folded sheet of writing paper, with a watermark dated 1868. 229 × 180 mm

Provenance: Mrs William Morris; May Morris; Dr Robert Steele, by whom bequeathed (see no. 25)

1941–9–1–4

Literature: S 744

On one side of the sheet, a winged bearded man holding a spear; on the other, a winged bird-like monster with a forked tail approaching a cliff on which is an army of soldiers with spears and shields.

24

25 'The Bard and Petty Tradesman'

Pen and brown ink. 116 × 175 mm

Inscribed with title, and below: *No. 1 London. Published as Lord Campbell's Act forbids. One Penny*

Provenance: Jane Morris; her daughter, May Morris; presented by Dr Robert Steele

1939−5−13−5

Literature: S 609

Drawn on the fourth page of a letter written on a sheet of folded writing-paper embossed with Rossetti's monogram and address. Dr Steele, who was executor of the will of William Morris's daughter May Morris, gave her mother's collection of caricature drawings, mostly of Morris, by Rossetti and Burne Jones to the Department of Prints and Drawings, and Rossetti's letters to Mrs Morris to the Department of Manuscripts of the British Museum (now the British Library), the latter with a restriction on publication until 1964. The present letter was overlooked by John Bryson and Janet Camp Troxell, *Dante Gabriel Rossetti and Jane Morris: Their Correspondence*, Oxford 1974, though the last part is quoted by Virginia Surtees. The full text reads:

16 Cheyne Walk
Friday [April/May 1868]

My dear Janey
I shall keep Wedy the 27th sacred to the Earthly Paradise. Will you tell Top that my soul expands to meet "large paper", but that meanwhile I extend my patronage forthwith to him and Ellis as one of the average public. I was touchingly reminded of his Eden today by the advent of asparagus at dinner. How each fresh article of food as it appears recalls the progress of the Poet's Year! Might not this afford a hint for a second series of Months if such is needed for part II ? As it is now the fashion for successful men in any walk of literature to start a newspaper at once, I offer overpage a heading on the principle of "The Globe and Traveller". Will you endeavour to make the "Great Original" seriously incline thereto ? Fancy the number of Editorial Chairs which would be smashed in the course of a week !

Yours affectionately
D. Gabriel R.

Another letter to Mrs Morris, dated 7 May 1868, was probably written very soon afterwards, for Rossetti refers to 'the bard and P.T. – I will not indulge him with his favourite

title' (Bryson and Troxell, p. 4, where the initials are misread as 'P. J.'), and asks her to tell Morris that he has 'not got any Earthly Paradise whatever at present'. The first part of Morris's *The Earthly Paradise*, a sequence of narrative poems grouped under the months of the year, was published by F.S. Ellis in April 1868. An edition of twenty-five 'large- or fine-paper' copies was later produced (see *William Morris and the Art of the Book*, New York, Pierpont Morgan Library, 1976, p. 117), and one was evidently promised to Rossetti, who in the meantime was to receive a copy of the ordinary commercial edition. The reference to the first asparagus confirms the suggested dating of the letter; and in 1868, May 27th fell on a Wednesday.

'The Great Original' is a phrase from Addison's hymn *The Spacious Firmament on High*. 'Petty Tradesman' refers to Morris's activity as founder of the decorating firm Morris, Marshall, Faulkner & Co. An act for the suppression of obscene publications was introduced by Lord Chief Justice Campbell in 1857.

26 'The M's at Ems'

Pen and brown ink. 112 × 179 mm

Inscribed with title lower r.

In the summer of 1869 concern for his wife's health led Morris to take her to try a 'cure' at the south German spa of Ems. Rossetti's drawing was enclosed in a letter of 21 July 1869 (Bryson and Troxell, letter 5) addressed to her in Cologne, en route for Ems, with the comment: 'The accompanying cartoon will prepare you for the worst. – which ever that may be, the seven tumblers or the 7 volumes [of *The Earthly Paradise*, which Morris is reading to her]'.

Provenance: as for no. 25

1939−5−13−1

Literature: S 605

The Bard

And Petty Tradesman.

NO I. London Published as Lord Campbell's Act forbids. One Penny

25

The M's at Ems

26

27 'The German Lesson'

Pen and brown ink. 145 × 178 mm

Inscribed with title

Provenance: as for no. 25

1939–5–13–2

Literature: S 603

The drawing accompanied a letter dated 4 August 1869 to Mrs Morris at Ems (Bryson and Troxell, letter 8), with the comment: 'I fear that the legitimate hopelessness of the pictorial and ideal Topsy has somewhat communicated itself to the German maid in the cartoon, and even you have rather a Georgian air. The poetry and philosophy of the subject are I hope complete, while you will see that even Scriptural analogy has not been neglected'. The last reference is to the picture on the wall entitled 'Das erdiges Paradies', of Adam proffering a fig-leaf to Eve. For 'The Earthly Paradise' see no. 25. 'Georgian' must be a reference to Burne Jones's wife Georgiana, always known as 'Georgie', whom he married in 1860.

28 'Resolution; or, The Infant Hercules'

Pen and brown ink. 205 × 131 mm

Inscribed with title and dated 14. 8. 69

Provenance: as for no. 25

1939–5–13–8

Literature: S 604

Inscribed with title, and in lower left corner, probably by Mrs Morris, 14. 8. 69, the date of the accompanying letter from Rossetti to her at Ems (Bryson and Troxell, letter 10) in which he says: 'Conceive if your cure were now to proceed so rapidly that there remained a glut of surplus baths, and Topsy were induced to express a thanksgiving frame of mind by that act which is next to godliness! Give him my love, and if he wishes to be revenged for the apposite diaphragm – i.e. diagram, let him know that I have bought the works of the poet Banting, that "idle singer of a too full day".'

William Banting in 1863 published *A Letter on Corpulence* in which he advocated dieting as a way of losing weight. The line 'The idle singer of an empty day' (i.e. the poet) occurs in Morris's then recently published poem *The Earthly Paradise*.

29 Rossetti lamenting the death of his Wombat

Pen and brown wash. 179 × 112 mm

Inscribed on the tomb: *6th November 1869*; and below:

I never reared a young Wombat
  To glad me with his pin-hole eye,
But when he most was sweet & fat
  And tail-less, he was sure to die.

Provenance: as for no. 25

1939–5–13–6

Literature: S 606

Rossetti was fascinated by exotic animals, and after moving to Chelsea in 1862 he installed a small menagerie in the garden of no. 16 Cheyne Walk. The wombat – 'a burrowing marsupial native to S. Australia and Tasmania, characterised by a thick heavy body, short legs, and a general resemblance to a small bear' – was a particular favourite and the source of many legends, some probably apocryphal (see Michael Archer, 'Rossetti and the Wombat' in *Apollo*, lxxxi (1965), pp. 178 ff.). In Oxford in 1857 Rossetti and Burne Jones amused themselves by making drawings of wombats; in a letter of 25 July 1860 he arranged to meet Madox Brown 'at the Zool. Gardens – place of meeting The Wombat's Lair'; in his sister Christina's poem *Goblin Market*, published in 1862, one of the goblins 'like a wombat prowled obtuse and furry'; and in his illustration to the poem, entitled 'Buy from us with a golden curl', the goblin in the foreground seems to be a wombat.

According to William Michael Rossetti (L & L, i, p. 253), 'The beasts upon which Dante's affections were prodigalized were the first wombat and his successor the woodchuck. The second wombat, having died immediately, accounts for little'. The drawing evidently commemorates the short-lived second wombat, for on 11 September 1869, only two months before the date inscribed on the tomb, Rossetti had written to Mrs Morris: 'What do you think? I

Resolution;
or, The Infant Hercules.

14·8·69

I never reared a young Wombat
To glad me with his pin-hole eye,
But when he most was sweet & fat
And tail-less, he was sure to die!

29

have got a Wombat at Chelsea, come the other day' (Bryson and Troxell, letter 14). A drawing by William Bell Scott in the Tate Gallery, dated 8 February 1871 and inscribed on the verso 'Rossetti's Wombat seated on his Lap', in fact represents the woodchuck.

The verse inscribed on the drawing is a parody of a passage in Thomas Moore's *Lalla Rookh*:

I never nurs'd a dear gazelle
  To glad me with its soft black eye,
But when it came to know me well
  And love me, it was sure to die!

30 Jane Morris leading the Wombat

Pen and brown ink. 179 × 112 mm

Provenance: as for no. 25

1939–5–13–3

Literature: S 607

See no. 29.

31 Morris fishing in a Punt

Pen and brown ink. 179 × 112 mm

Inscribed by Rossetti:

Enter Morris moored in a punt,
And Jacks and Tenches exeunt. Kelmscott 11 Sept 1871

Provenance: as for no. 25

1939–5–13–9

Literature: S 608

In a letter to William Bell Scott dated 'Kelmscott 15 September', Rossetti describes Morris's return from Iceland and continues: 'One day he was here he went for a day's fishing in our punt, the chief result of which was a sketch I made, inscribed as follows [as above, with 'Skald', the ancient Icelandic word for poet, substituted for 'Morris']'.

30

Kelmscott
11 Sept 1871

Enter Morris, moored in a punt,
And Jacks & Tenches exeunt.

31

32 'Rupes Topseia'

Pen and brown ink. 179 × 112 mm

Provenance: as for no. 25

1939–5–13–7

Literature: S 611

The title, inscribed by Rossetti lower right, is a reference to Morris's nickname of 'Topsy' and to the *Rupes Tarpeia* (the Tarpeian Rock) on the Capitoline Hill in Rome, one side of which was a precipice from which condemned criminals were thrown to their deaths. Morris's spectacles are falling with him, together with a copy of *The Earthly Paradise* and a knife and fork (presumably in allusion to his love of food: see nos. 65 and 66). At the top of the hill is a ruinous temple having on the broken entablature the end of an inscription . . . *& Co.* In front sit a row of six figures, among them Rossetti, Burne Jones, Madox Brown and the architect Philip Webb, all partners in the firm of Morris, Marshall, Faulkner & Co.; the other two are presumably their fellow-partners Paul Marshall and C. J. Faulkner. Between them they hold a banner inscribed *WE ARE STARVING*. Mrs Morris in the crescent moon looks down on the scene; below her, framed by the sun, are the heads of two bearded men, one wearing spectacles and the other an eyeglass, and a dove apparently cocking a snook at Morris with its claw.

In 1874 Morris proposed to take entire control of the firm by buying out his partners, a proposal much resented by some of them, especially Rossetti and Madox Brown. In this drawing Rossetti's annoyance is humorously expressed, but Morris's action ultimately led to a permanent breach between them. The drawing cannot be fully elucidated until the two bearded heads in the sun are identified. Virginia Surtees ingeniously suggested that they might be Karl Marx and Friedrich Engels, but it was not until the 1880s that Morris became seriously involved in socialist politics.

33 Mrs Morris on a Sofa

Black chalk and pencil. 343 × 423 mm (image), 352 × 461 mm (sheet)

Inscribed by the draughtsman in pencil: *27 July 1870*

Provenance: Mrs Morris; given by her as a wedding present to Theodore and Clara Watts-Dunton in 1905; Mrs Watts-Dunton (sale, Sotheby's, 17 March 1939, lot 62), bought Barbizon House (£28); Cecil French, by whom bequeathed

1954–5–8–4

Literature: M 229 (medium incorrectly given as pen and ink); S 380

On a label detached from the back of the frame is written, in Cecil French's favourite violet ink: *This, coming from the Watts-Dunton sale, had been looked at for many years by the green eyes of A.C.S. Cecil French, June 1945.* From 1879 onwards the poet Algernon Charles Swinburne lived in Theodore Watts-Dunton's house in Putney, but the drawing would have been under his eyes for less than four years. It was not given to the Watts-Duntons until 1905, and Swinburne died in April 1909.

34 Mrs Morris reclining on a Sofa

Pen and brown ink. 283 × 437 mm

Inscribed by the draughtsman in pencil: *6 January 1872*

1954–5–8–2 Bequeathed by Cecil French

Literature: S 393

27 July 1870

33

6th January 1872

35 Half-length Figures of a Man and a Woman embracing

Pencil, over traces of underdrawing in red chalk.
239 × 290 mm

Provenance: probably Rossetti Sale, Christie's, 12 May 1883, lot 199 or 200; David Gould; in 1949 exchanged with Cecil French, by whom bequeathed

1954–5–8–5

Literature: S 244J

A study for one of the pairs of embracing lovers in the background of *The Blessed Damozel* (Fogg Museum, Harvard), which Rossetti agreed in December 1873 to paint for William Graham, and which he completed in the spring of 1877.

36 Orpheus and Eurydice in Hades, with Pluto and Proserpine

Pencil. 610 × 514 mm

Provenance: Rossetti Sale, Christie's, 12 May 1883, lot 180; Colonel Gillum, by whom bequeathed

1910–12–10–9

Literature: M 223; S 243

Pluto, the god of the Underworld, allowed Orpheus to restore his wife Eurydice to life on condition that he did not look back at her while conducting her out of Hades. The drawing shows the moment when Orpheus ignores the condition.

No corresponding painting is known, and in a letter to his friend Thomas Gordon Hake, dated 20 July 1875, Rossetti says: 'I have struck about among fresh ideas before commencing some new picture, but commissions must be met, and to fit picture to price is not always quite easy. Meanwhile I now and then launch into a design irrespective of contingencies, and should like to show you one I am now making of *Orpheus and Eurydice*.'

36

John Everett Millais

(1829–1896)

An infant prodigy, Millais was only ten years old when he qualified for admission to the Royal Academy Schools; and his painting of *Pizarro seizing the Inca of Peru* (Victoria and Albert Museum) in the conventional academic style of the time is a remarkable achievement for a boy of sixteen. In 1848 he, Holman Hunt and Rossetti combined to found the Pre-Raphaelite Brotherhood. *Lorenzo and Isabella* (see no. 37), shown at the RA in the following year, was the first of a series exhibited in the 1850s, including *Ferdinand and Ariel*, *Christ in the House of his Parents*, *Ophelia*, *John Ruskin*, *Autumn Leaves*, *The Blind Girl*, in which the principles of Pre-Raphaelitism were expressed in a technique of dazzling virtuosity. But (as happened even more conspicuously with Arthur Hughes) the high level of technique and emotional intensity could not be sustained. By the end of the decade the quality of Millais's imaginative work began to decline, though his technical skill always gives it a certain distinction, and in the 1860s he designed some of the most beautiful book-illustrations of the period. Of his later paintings the best are his numerous portraits. Millais's career was one of unbroken success. Elected ARA as early as 1853 (RA 1863), he was created a baronet in 1885, and in his later years is said to have had an income of £30,000 a year. In 1896, though a dying man, his supremacy was acknowledged by his election to succeed Frederic Leighton as President of the Royal Academy, an honour which he enjoyed for only a few months.

37 Lorenzo and Isabella

Pencil. 225 × 310mm

Inscribed top l.: *passion flower*; and lower r.: *very thin page*

1901–5–16–10 Purchased from the Fine Art Society

Literature: LB 3; Millais Exh., RA 1967, no. 229; Bennett, Merseyside Colls. Cat., 1988, p. 119, fig. 51

A sketch for the painting in the Walker Art Gallery, Liverpool, dated 1849, the first that Millais exhibited after the foundation of the Pre-Raphaelite Brotherhood in September 1848. It was clearly intended as a manifesto of the ideals of the Brotherhood: not only did he add the then mysterious initials *PRB* to his signature, but also incorporated them in the carved decoration of the bench-end on the right of the table.

The subject is from Keats's poem *Isabella, or the Pot of Basil*, derived from a story by Boccaccio. Isabella and Lorenzo, a humble clerk in her brothers' prosperous business, fall in love. The brothers violently object, and resolve the situation by murdering him. The drawing includes all the essential elements of the composition in its final form: the two brothers sitting opposite the lovers, one narrowly scrutinising them, the other, brutally kicking Isabella's dog, with the extended leg which is the most striking feature of the composition.

The first inscription is explained by reference to the painting, in which a passion flower on the pillar of the balcony is visible immediately above Isabella's head – a characteristic example of Pre-Raphaelite symbolism; the other must refer to the physique of the servant (or 'page') who stands behind her on the extreme right.

37

38 A Lady in a Garden cutting a Flower from a Trellis

Pencil, on a fragment of an etching. 288 × 116 mm (arched top)

1901–5–16–9 Purchased from the Fine Art Society

Literature: LB 4; J.G. Millais, i, p. 51

Reproduced by J. G. Millais with the caption 'Design for Pre-Raphaelite Etching intended for *The Germ*, 1849'. The short-lived periodical *The Germ: Thoughts towards Nature in Poetry, Literature and Art* was founded, mainly on the initiative of Rossetti, to expound and publicise the aims of the Pre-Raphaelite Brotherhood. Contributors were not confined to members of the Brotherhood: they included Christina Rossetti, Madox Brown, Coventry Patmore, W. H. Deverell (see p. 8) and William Bell Scott (see p. 132). Each of the four numbers, which appeared between January and May 1850, was illustrated with an etching, respectively by Holman Hunt, Collinson, Madox Brown and Deverell. Millais may well have contemplated making an illustration, but it may be doubted whether this was the purpose of the present drawing. The high narrow shape of the composition with its arched top – not the result of later trimming but deliberately indicated with framing-lines – would have fitted awkwardly on to an octavo page. The Pre-Raphaelites often gave their pictures shaped tops suggestive of *trecento* panel paintings, and it seems more likely that this is a sketch for a small picture. The dating 1849/50 is certainly correct.

The fragment of an etching along the lower part of the right edge of the drawing is not by Millais. It seems to represent a row of railings and the upper part of a gate-pier.

39 The Eve of the Deluge

Pen and Indian ink, with some grey wash, over pencil. Squared in pencil. 240 × 413 mm

1901–5–16–8 Purchased from the Fine Art Society

Literature: LB 2; J.G.Millais, i, pp. 91, 94–5, 103–5; Millais Drawings Exh., Arts Council 1979, no. 47; Tate Exh., 1984, no. 171, repr.

The careful precision and delicacy of such of the drawing as is finished suggest that it was intended as a work complete in itself. On the other hand, it is squared as if for enlargement, and in a letter dated 28 [May?] 1851 to his confidante in Oxford, the wife of his early patron Thomas Combe of the Clarendon Press, Millais describes the subject as that of 'the picture I have in contemplation'. If he began with the intention of making a finished drawing and later changed his mind, this would explain why he abandoned the drawing before completely inking over the preliminary pencil sketch. In an earlier letter, dated 2 December 1850, he had told her 'I have entirely settled the composition of the Flood and shall commence it this week'; but on 28 January 1851 he says that he has given it up 'for this year, and have substituted a smaller composition [i.e. *The Return of the Dove to the Ark*, now in the Ashmolean Museum, Oxford]'. Three years later, on 7 February 1854, he wrote to Holman Hunt of his intention of joining him in the Holy Land in the autumn. 'I shall begin The Flood, which I shall be able to paint any-where, and take about with me'.

'I shall endeavour' he told Mrs Combe, 'to affect those who may look on it with the awful uncertainty of life and the necessity of always being prepared for death'. The composition described would have been more elaborate than the drawing: 'My intention is to lay the scene at the marriage feast. The bride, elated by her happiness, will be playfully showing her wedding-ring to a young girl who will be in the act of plighting her troth to a man wholly engrossed in his love, the parents of each uniting in congratulation at the consummation of their own and their children's happiness'.

So far, the description tallies with the drawing, but there is no sign of the 'drunkard railing boisterously at another less intoxicated, for his cowardice in being somewhat appalled at the view the open window presents'. The man with the

38

39

dog in the left foreground of the drawing has not yet become 'the glutton quietly indulging in his weakness, unheeding the sagacity of his grateful dog, who, thrusting his head under his hands to attract attention, instinctively feels the coming ruin'; nor has the figure clutching her skirt next to him become 'the woman (typical of worldly vanity), apparelled in sumptuous attire, withholding her robes from the contamination of [the dog's] dripping hide', since the dog is on the far side of the table. The 'one figure in their midst, who, upright with closed eyes, prays for mercy for those around her, a patient example of belief standing with, but far from, them, placidly awaiting God's will' would have developed from the concerned-looking woman in the background who gesticulates towards the window.

40 Head and Shoulders of a Young Girl, three-quarters to left: Ann Lynn

Watercolour over pencil. 220 × 191 mm

Signed lower l. with monogram, and dated *1852*

Provenance: Eric Millar, by whom bequeathed 1967–10–14–124

Literature: Millais Drawings Exh., Arts Council 1979, no. 16

See no. 41.

40

41

41 Head and Shoulders of a Young Girl, full-face: Fanny Lynn

Watercolour over pencil. 214 × 187 mm

Signed lower l. with monogram, and dated *1852*

Provenance: as for no. 40

1967–10–14–126

Literature: Millais Drawings Exh., Arts Council 1979, no. 17

The names of the sitters are given in the departmental register of acquisitions, and were presumably taken from a label or inscription formerly on the frame or mount. Malcolm Warner suggests that they may have been daughters of the 'Lynn' who in June 1852 made 'a regular artist's shooting-stool, shutting up and portable' for Millais when he was at Hayes in Kent painting the background of *The Proscribed Royalist* (J. G. Millais, i, p. 168). A third drawing of the group, of Fanny in profile to left, in a private collection, was no. 18 in the Millais Drawings Exh., 1979.

42 Humorous Drawing: Sporting Gent and Highland Boy

Pen and pale brown ink, on sheet of writing paper. 179 × 111 mm

Signed with monogram and dated *1853* and inscribed: *Sporting gent – I say my boy, how did you get those birds?/ Highland boy – I just killed it wi a stane*

1979–4–7–13 Purchased from Langton Gallery through the Oppenheimer Fund

Literature: Millais Exh., RA 1967, no. 313; Mary Lutyens and Malcolm Warner, *Rainy Days at Brig o'Turk* (1983), p. 79, no. 40

Millais spent the summer and autumn of 1853 in Scotland with the Ruskins for the purpose of painting Ruskin's portrait. He recorded the adventures of the party in a series of drawings which constituted a kind of pictorial diary. Some of them were illustrated by J. G. Millais, and the whole series by Mary Lutyens and Malcolm Warner in 1983.

Not long before he left for Scotland, Millais had made friends with John Leech, the draughtsman now best remembered for his humorous drawings in *Punch* and his illustrations to the novels of R. S. Surtees. In the autumn of 1853 he sent six of his Scottish drawings, including no. 42, to Leech, as possibly being suitable for *Punch* (the others are Lutyens and Warner nos. 39 and 41–44), with the stipulation that his name should not appear 'which would never go with the serious position which I occupy in regard to Art' (Millais Drawings Exh., Arts Council 1979, p. 10)

In the event, only two were engraved and published: *This is the protection a plaid affords to those who do not know the way to carry it* (15 October) and *Awful protection against midges* (12 November). The present drawing, though a typical example of the *Punch* humour of the period, was not used. Millais himself seems to have had some misgivings about it, for in his letter to Leech he says: 'The sketch of the sportsman I am afraid does not quite tell its story. The fact is that for some time past our table has been furnished with game by little boys who seem to be cunning throwers, but in truth I believe their papas lay snares for birds and get their children to release them in the morning and in answer to all enquiries are told to say they killed them with a stone.'.

Sporting gent – I say my boy, how did you get those birds ?
Highland boy – I just killed it wi a stane...

18 53

42

43 Married for Love

Pen and black ink, with some grey wash and some brown ink. 246 × 174 mm

Inscribed with monogram and dated *1853*

Provenance: William Reed (according to J. G. Millais); by descent to Richard Palmer (sale, Christie's, 12 December 1972, lot 46); bought Colnaghi, from whom purchased

1976–10–30–32

Literature: J. G. Millais, ii, p. 490; Millais Commemorative Exh., RA, 1898, no. 235; Millais Drawings Exh., Arts Council 1979, no. 19; Tate Exh., 1984, no. 189

One of the group of 'modern life' subjects of 1853–4 (see no. 8). The eight illustrated by J. G. Millais are listed by him as belonging to George Gray, Lady Millais's brother. These are: *Accepted*, *Rejected*, *The Dying Man* and *The Blind Man* (Yale Center for British Art), *The Race Meeting* (Ashmolean Museum), *The Ghost* (Victoria and Albert Museum), *Retribution* (British Museum, no. 44), and *Virtue and Vice* (Mr Raoul Millais). Also illustrated is *The Romans leaving Britain* (whereabouts unknown), dated 1853 like most of the series and resembling them exactly in technique and sentiment; but the only drawing of the subject listed, also as belonging to George Gray, is under the date 1849 and described as 'A highly finished drawing done for the Cyclographic Club . . . the artist afterwards carried out this picture in a large work in oils, altering the design only slightly'. There is no other record of such a painting.

Married for Love and its two companions *Married for Rank* (Mr and Mrs Harold Wernick) and *Married for Money* (private collection) did not belong to George Gray. All three are reproduced in the catalogue of the Millais Drawings Exhibition, Arts Council 1979 (nos. 19, 20, 21, and Tate Exh., 1984, nos. 189, 187, 188). J. G. Millais does not illustrate them and may not even have seen them, for though they are in the same technique as the rest of the series, he describes them as being in 'pen and ink washed with colour'. Furthermore, he includes among the drawings belonging to George Gray one of a 'woman in church, watching her former lover married'. The description corre-

sponds with *Married for Money*, an etching of which was used to illustrate an edition of Moore's *Irish Melodies* published in 1856; in this connexion it may have been necessary to make a repetition, which could have come into George Gray's possession, but if so it has disappeared.

44 'Retribution'

Pen and brown ink. 201 × 256 mm (image), 214 × 275 mm (sheet)

Signed with monogram and dated *1854*

Provenance: Lady Millais (the artist's wife); her brother, George Gray; Melville Gray; Mrs Sophie McEwen; Miss Veronica McEwen; E. G. Millais (the artist's grandson); his sale, Christie's, 20 March 1979, lot 208, bought J. S. Maas, from whom purchased

1982–12–11–1

Literature: J. G. Millais, i, p. 227 and ii, p. 490; Fine Art Society Exh., London, 1901, no. 77; Ironside & Gere, p. 41, pl. 59; Millais Exh., RA 1967, no. 334; T. Hilton, *The Pre-Raphaelites* (1970), p. 140, repr.; Tate Exh., 1984, no. 194, repr.

This and no. 43 above belong to a series of eleven drawings of scenes from contemporary life, eight of which are inscribed with the date 1853. Seven of the series deal with themes of courtship or marriage, melodramatically in the present drawing and in *The Ghost* (Victoria & Albert Museum), of a bride at the altar about to accept the ring and recoiling at the ghostly apparition of a former lover. 'Unconsecrated passion in modern life', to use Holman Hunt's expression, is also treated in *The Race-Meeting* (Ashmolean Museum), in which a 'swell' with his weeping mistress by his side leans nonchalantly back in his carriage and announces his inability to pay his gambling debts; and in *Virtue and Vice* (private collection), a prostitute exhorting a virtuous seamstress to abandon her poor but honest livelihood. Also dated 1853, and identical in technique, style and sentiment, though not of a contemporary subject, is the drawing of *The Romans leaving Britain* (whereabouts unknown: repr. J. G. Millais, i, p. 199), in which a legionary about to embark is passionately embracing the woman he is forced to leave behind.

This group of drawings is the equivalent of Rossetti's and Holman Hunt's 'modern life' subjects *Found* and *The Awakening Conscience*, also works of the years 1853–4 (see no. 8). Millais's intention 'to have shown by illustration the various tragedies of sin and temptation which assail the lot of man', is expressed in the same sententious vein as his exposition of the theme of *The Eve of the Deluge* (see no. 39), but a less impersonal motive lay behind his temporary obsession with these various aspects of sexual passion. In 1853 he found himself falling deeply, and as it then seemed hopelessly, in love with Mrs Ruskin. There was nothing of the Bohemian in him, and for so conventional and moralistic a young man this must have been a deeply disturbing experience (see Mary Lutyens, *Millais and the Ruskins*, 1965). But the annulment of Mrs Ruskin's marriage in 1854 left her free to marry Millais. In *The Romans leaving Britain*, the most emotionally charged of the whole series, the woman's face resembles hers.

The title 'Retribution' was probably invented by the artist's son and biographer. His alternative title, 'The Man with Two Wives', is incorrect, for the left hand of the seated woman so conspicuously placed on the man's right knee is ringless, and she indicates with her other hand the wedding ring worn by the kneeling woman.

A better title might be 'The Foiled Bigamist'. A dissolute 'swell', of the type of those in *The Race-Meeting* and *The Awakening Conscience*, engaged to marry a beautiful and in every way suitable young lady of his own rank in life, is disconcerted on the morning of the wedding by the appearance of a woman whom he had married some years before and by whom he has had two children. The contrast between the reactions of the boy and girl is a nice psychological touch. The prospective bride seems to be wearing a wedding-dress, and the pile of bouquets on the table must have been placed there in readiness for the bridesmaids. (The convention that bride and groom should not see one another on their wedding-day until they meet at the altar was not observed in the mid-nineteenth century. When Queen Victoria was married in 1840 she recorded in her journal that on the morning of the wedding she 'Had my hair dressed and the wreath of orange flowers put on. Saw Albert for the *last* time *alone*, as my *Bridegroom*.' The bride in the drawing is not wearing an engagement ring, but this too was a fashion that did not come in until later in the century.

It has been suggested, largely on the grounds that a picture of a ballet dancer would have been an unlikely ornament in a respectable English home, that the seated woman is the mistress. But (a) she does not look like a mistress, (b) a mistress would not be horrified, or even surprised, to learn that her lover is married, and (c) the hat and gloves on the floor show that the man is paying a formal and ceremonious call.

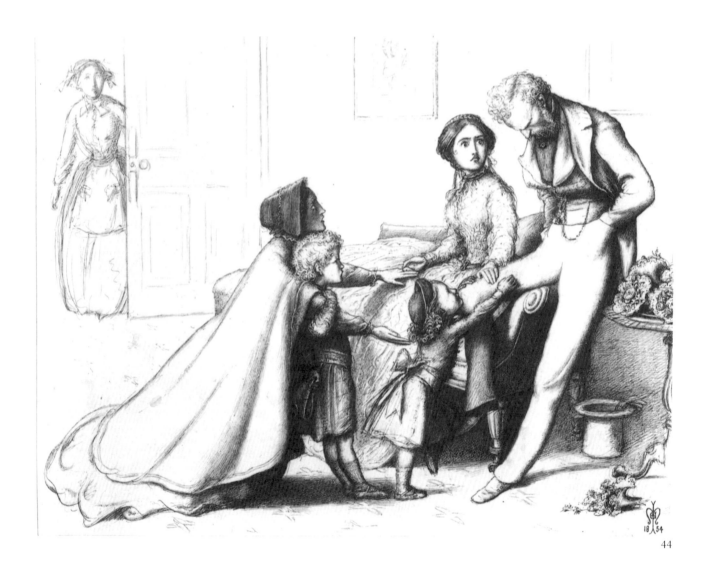

44

John Everett Millais

45

46

45 Sketches for *Peace Concluded, 1856*

Pencil. 162 × 226mm

1901–5–16–15 *Purchased from the Fine Art Society*

Literature: LB 5b

46 Composition Study for *Peace Concluded, 1856*

Pencil. 228 × 178mm

Inscribed in pencil top l., by the draughtsman: *Violet velvet/ Times newspaper Peace/ Noah's ark*

1901–5–16–14 Purchased from the Fine Art Society

Literature: LB 5a; Michael Hancher, *Burlington Magazine*, 1991, p. 501, fig. 15

The painting was exhibited at the Royal Academy in 1856 and is now in the Minneapolis Institute of Arts (Hancher, fig. 14). An officer invalided from the Crimea, at home with his wife and two small daughters, holds in his hand *The Times* of 31 March 1856 open at the page with the announcement of the signature of the Treaty of Paris and the formal conclusion of hostilities between Russia on one hand and Great Britain, France and Turkey on the other. The topical subject and banal sentiment made it an instant success. Millais sold it for the then very large price of 900 guineas, while for the other painting he exhibited, *Autumn Leaves* (Manchester), now regarded as one of his masterpieces, he received only £700. Ruskin predicted that both 'would rank . . . among the world's best masterpieces' (*Works*, vol. xiv, pp. 56–7).

No. 46 corresponds in all essentials with the finished picture, including even the shallow arched top drawn over the original rectangular shape. The main difference is that the child on the left is holding the Noah's Ark which in the painting is on the floor at her feet; her sister is also in a different position. The creature above is the dog which in the painting appears on the extreme right, lying on the couch on which its master and mistress are sitting.

Two earlier solutions are sketched on no. 45, a spread-out sheet of folded, highly glazed, writing-paper. In the first, the officer is seated on the right, facing the spectator; his wife kneels to the left, with her head lowered and her hands on his right thigh. The second solution was drawn over it with a heavier amd more emphatic touch, with the sheet the other way up. The officer, wearing a kilt, is reclining on a couch with his legs extended to left; his wife, kneeling by his side, rests her head on his left arm, while he grasps her left shoulder with his right hand. What could be the head of a figure kneeling at the head of the couch is roughly indicated.

The inclusion of the date 1856 in the title, and the careful rendering of the newspaper so that the headline 'Conclusion of Peace' is legible (Hancher, fig. 19), emphasise the subject so unequivocally, and so obviously, that it is surprising to find Millais's fellow Pre-Raphaelite Brother, F. G. Stephens, being so obtuse as to interpret it as 'a matrimonial reconciliation'. In his article, entitled 'Urgent Private Affairs', Mr Hancher discusses the nature of Millais's original intention. Both Holman Hunt in his reminiscences, *Pre-Raphaelitism and the Pre-Raphaelite Brotherhood* (1905), and Ford Madox Brown in his journal for 11 April 1856, say that Millais had originally intended a satire on the way in which some officers in the Crimea unjustifiably claimed home leave, but that the war ended before it was finished and 'the painter adroitly adapted his work to the changing circumstances'. Millais may well have contemplated such a subject and discussed it with his friends; but X-rays of the picture reveal no signs of last-minute change, and the study for the whole composition (no. 46) shows that it was complete in his head when he began painting, including the newspaper. Mr Hancher does not mention the earlier sketches (no. 45), in which the officer's reclining pose shows unmistakably that he is an invalid.

47

47 'A Lost Love'

Watercolour. 103 × 85 mm

Signed lower l. with monogram

Provenance: Sydney Morse (sale, Christie's, 19 March 1937, lot 124); presented by L.G. Esmond Morse in memory of his father

1937–4–10–3

A wood-engraving of this composition, signed by Dalziel, appeared in *Once a Week* on 3 December 1859 (p. 482) illustrating 'A Lost Love', a poem signed with the initials 'R.A.B.' It is unnecessary to quote more than the first stanza:

So fair and yet so desolate;
   So wan, and yet so young;
Oh, there is quiet too deep for tears,
   Too seal'd for tell-tale tongue!
With a faded floweret in her hand,
   Poor little hand, so white!
And dim blue eye, from her casement high
   She looks upon the night.

The watercolour corresponds exactly with the wood-engraving, and is on exactly the same scale and in the same direction. It is not a preliminary study, but a later version.

Thomas Woolner
(1825–1892)

Of the seven members of the Pre-Raphaelite Brotherhood, Woolner was alone in being a sculptor. Holman Hunt records that Rossetti was impressed by his agreement with his own and Millais's 'resolution to turn more devotedly to nature as the means of purifying modern art . . . [he] had declared the system to be the only one that could reform sculpture, and that therefore he wished to be enrolled with us'. Pre-Raphaelite painting ideally represented some crisis of conscience, either a state of exalted emotional tension or of high moral purport, enhanced in intensity by a degree of realism so highly burnished as to seem almost hallucinatory. This ideal cannot be fully expressed in the more formal and abstract medium of sculpture, especially in the middle of the nineteenth century when the activity of sculptors was largely confined to portraiture. Nevertheless, as Ben Read has convincingly argued ('Was there Pre-Raphaelite Sculpture?' in *Pre-Raphaelite Papers*, 1984), 'the combination of High Seriousness and Naturalism' in Woolner's portrait busts and medallions and whole-length figures, and such ideal groups as the *Mother and Child* at Wallington Hall, is fully consonant with the ideals of Pre-Raphaelitism.

Woolner's verse would have been a further recommendation to Rossetti. If there is such a thing as a specifically Pre-Raphaelite school of poetry, the term would certainly apply to his long poem 'My Beautiful Lady' (published in full in 1863), part of which appeared in the first number of *The Germ* in 1850 illustrated with an etching by Holman Hunt. In 1852, when Woolner emigrated to Australia in the vain hope of making a fortune in the goldfields, Madox Brown was one of the party who saw him off at Gravesend, an episode which inspired the painting *The Last of England*. Woolner returned in 1854, and resumed his career, receiving many distinguished public commissions. He was elected ARA in 1871 and RA in 1874.

48 A Shepherd Boy with his Dog, playing a Pipe

Pencil. 266 × 176mm

Inscribed with date *1861*

1941–12–13–527 Presented by the Reverend Francis and Miss Annora Palgrave

This drawing, though quite un-Pre-Raphaelite in character, is included because Woolner was one of the original members of the Pre-Raphaelite Brotherhood. It is a design for the vignette on the title-page of F. T. Palgrave's *Golden Treasury of the Best Songs and Lyrical Poems in the English Language*, first published by Macmillan in 1861.

48

George Price Boyce
(1826–1897)

Boyce originally intended to be an architect, but after three years as an articled pupil chose instead to be a painter. At the same time, in about 1849, he came to know Rossetti, who was to remain an intimate friend for the next thirty years. Boyce confined himself to watercolour landscape, to which he applied strict Pre-Raphaelite principles of truth to nature. He found many of his subjects in the mellow landscape of the upper Thames valley, and he excelled in the representation of old red brickwork (as in no. 51). Well enough off to make a large collection of Rossetti's works (Virginia Surtees lists more than forty that once belonged to him), he did not depend on his art for a livelihood, but his work is of fully professional standard. Even in the rigorously edited form insisted upon by his family, the diary which he kept between 1851 and 1875 (the complete manuscript was destroyed by enemy action in 1942) is a lively document, important for its references to Rossetti.

Literature: 'The Diaries of George Price Boyce', ed. Randall Davies, in *The Old Watercolour Society's Nineteenth Annual Volume* (1941); text reprinted photographically, with notes etc. by Virginia Surtees (Real World, Norwich, 1980); Christopher Newall and Judy Egerton, *George Price Boyce* (Exh. Tate Gallery, 1987).

49 A Farmhouse at Streatley-on-Thames

Watercolour. 135 × 387 mm

Signed lower l. and dated *June 59*

Provenance: Colonel Gillum (bought from the artist in 1860); bequeathed by Mrs Gillum

1915–2–13–2

Literature: British Landscape Watercolours Exh., BM 1985, no. 188; Boyce Exh., Tate 1987, no. 26; Nature into Art Exh., BM 1991, no. 94 (colour repr.)

Boyce recorded in his journal on 27 February 1860 that 'Major Gillum paid me 16 gns. for the drawing done at Streatley of the long-grass meadow and mowers'.

49

50 'Backs of some old houses in Soho'

Watercolour on two pieces of paper joined together.
184 × 189 mm (sight)

Signed along lower edge and dated *April 26th 1866*

Provenance: D. G. Rossetti (sale, T. G. Wharton, Martin & Co. at 16 Cheyne Walk, 6 July 1882, lot 310); C. F. Bell (who records buying it for his father at a sale at Phillips in New Bond St. on 3 October 1893), by whom presented

1942–10–10–9

Literature: Reviewed in *Athenaeum*, 1 December 1866, p. 721; British Landscape Watercolours Exh., BM 1985, no. 189; Boyce Exh., Tate 1987, no. 45

The drawing is still on C. F. Bell's mount with his annotations on the back together with a label from the previous frame (described by him, with characteristic exactitude, as 'a ¾ inch plain gold moulding with a 2¾ inch gold flat inside'), on which Boyce had written the title as given above and his name and address (*14 Chatham Place, Blackfriars*), and Rossetti his (*16 Cheyne Walk, Chelsea*). In his diary on 21 May 1866 Boyce records that Rossetti 'took a fancy to the little watercolour sketch I made in Prince's Street, Soho, some weeks ago, and offered a sketch of his for it. I closed, of course'; in the event (as he recorded on 10 March 1867) Rossetti gave him three drawings (S 62D, 532, 533).

An inscription by Boyce on the verso, 'from a 1st floor of a house overlooking the churchyard of St Anne's', is transcribed by Bell, who adds 'The place where this view was taken was no doubt the room over the shop of Ford and Dickinson, carvers and gilders, at 90 Wardour Street'. Before the construction of Shaftesbury Avenue in the 1880s the southern end of the present Wardour Street, between Old Compton Street and Coventry Street, was known as Princes Street.

51 'Mr Buckingham's House, Dorchester'

COLOUR PLATE II

Watercolour. 263 × 193 mm

Signed lower l. and dated *Sept 1869*, with title, signature and date inscribed in pencil on the verso. Also on the verso are two separate studies in pencil of the initials *IPM* and the date *1737* with a note: *carved (projecting) upon brickwork of parapet*

Provenance: John James Stevenson (see below); purchased from Stephen Somerville

1991–10–5–2

This drawing played a part in the propagation of the 'Queen Anne Revival', the preferred architectural style of the Aesthetic Movement of the 1870s and 1880s (see M. Girouard, *Sweetness and Light: The Queen Anne Movement 1860–1900*, 1977). In his journal on June 20 1872, Boyce recorded: 'Called upon Mr Robson and Mr J. J. Stevenson about the proposed School Board school next door to me. Mr Stevenson produced my "Back of an Old House, Dorchester" drawing, which seemed to be in his office for the sake of making people who would otherwise prefer purple slates on drab stocks [i.e. London stock brick, usually brown or dirty yellow] and cement and thin window bars and plate glass, swallow red tiles and red brick and thick window bars'. Early examples of the Queen Anne style are Boyce's own house in Chelsea, completed in 1871 to the design of Philip Webb, and the house formerly in the Bayswater Road which J. J. Stevenson built for himself in 1871–3. Robson and Stevenson were appointed architects to the London School Board in 1871 and devised a simplified form of 'Queen Anne' for their schools. Given its dissimilar scale and different function, the school designed by them in Upper Cheyne Walk is an unexpectedly harmonious next-door neighbour to Boyce's house in Glebe Place.

50

PLATE I

(Above)
10 Dante Gabriel Rossetti:
Arthur's Tomb

(Right)
112 James Smetham:
'*The Knight's Bridal*'

PLATE II

(Above)
95 Walter Crane:
A Stream in a Wood

(Left)
51 George Price Boyce:
'Mr Buckingham's House,
Dorchester'

(Right, above)
101 William Henry
Millais:
A Scottish Farmstead

(Right, below)
103 John William North:
Halsway Court, Somerset

PLATE V

(Left)
58 Edward Burne Jones:
Cupid finding Psyche

(Right)
96 Henry Holiday:
*Two Women in Sixteenth-
Century Costume*

PLATE VI

(Above)
107 William Bell Scott:
King Edward's Bay

(Left)
76 George, Earl of
Carlisle:
*Two Ladies under a
Pergola below a Cliff*

(Right)
104 John Ruskin:
*A Rock covered with Ivy
and Lichen*

PLATE VII

PLATE VIII

52 John Brett: *Pansies and Fern-Shoots*

PLATE III

PLATE IV

John Brett
(1830–1902)

Brett's reputation rests on a few landscapes painted in the 1850s, especially *The Glacier of Rosenlaui* (1856, Tate Gallery), *The Stonebreaker* (1856–7, Birmingham) and *The Val d'Aosta* (1857, private collection): extraordinary *tours de force* which carry to its ultimate limit the Ruskinian principle that the artist's duty is to portray nature exactly as she is, adding nothing and subtracting nothing. The strain of the intense concentration required proved too much for Brett, whose later paintings, often of seashore subjects, tend to be dry and pedantic.

52 Pansies and Fern-shoots

COLOUR PLATE VIII

Watercolour and bodycolour. 153 × 146 mm

Signed lower l.: *J.B. 1862*

1994–6–18–1 Purchased from Stephen Somerville

Ruskin admired Brett's early landscapes, and advised and encouraged him over *The Val d'Aosta*, which he eventually purchased. This intense little 'close-up' of a detail of a landscape is entirely in his spirit. One of Brett's exhibits in the 1857 Pre-Raphaelite exhibition in Russell Place was 'Moss and Gentian, from the Engels Horner'.

Ford Madox Brown
(1821–1893)

Madox Brown was some years older than Hunt, Rossetti and Millais, and by the time he met them in 1848 had already had the benefit of a cosmopolitan training: at the Antwerp Academy under Baron Wappers, in Paris, and in Rome, where he came to know Cornelius and Overbeck, the surviving members of the German 'Early Christian' or 'Nazarene' group. Some of his early work reflects these varied influences: *The Execution of Mary Queen of Scots* (1841/2) suggests knowledge of Delaroche, while *Wycliff reading his Translation of the Bible to John of Gaunt* (1848) has a Nazarene flavour. In 1848 Rossetti, having decided that his own life-work should be painting and not poetry, wrote to Madox Brown expressing admiration for his work and asking if he would take him as a pupil. The apprenticeship did not last long, for the pupil soon tired of the master's elementary but thorough method of training, but the two became, and remained, lifelong and intimate friends. Though not invited to join the Pre-Raphaelite Brotherhood – no doubt he was felt to be too old and experienced to want to take part in a students' society – he contributed to *The Germ* in 1850, and from the beginning was one of the inner circle. His slowly pondered pictures of the 1850s, such as '*Take your Son, Sir*' (begun 1851), *The Pretty Baa-Lambs* (begun 1851), *Work* (begun 1852) and *The Last of England* (begun 1852), are entirely Pre-Raphaelite in style and technique. So too is the group of 'pure' landscapes, including *An English Autumn Afternoon* (begun 1852), *Carrying Corn* (1854–5), *The Hayfield* (1855–6) and *Hampstead from my Window* (1857). In the 1860s his work began to be influenced by the later style of Rossetti, and, not altogether to its advantage, became increasingly sensuous and romantic. The diary which Madox Brown kept between 1847 and 1858 is one of the most interesting and informative of Pre-Raphaelite original documents (ed. Virginia Surtees, Yale, 1981).

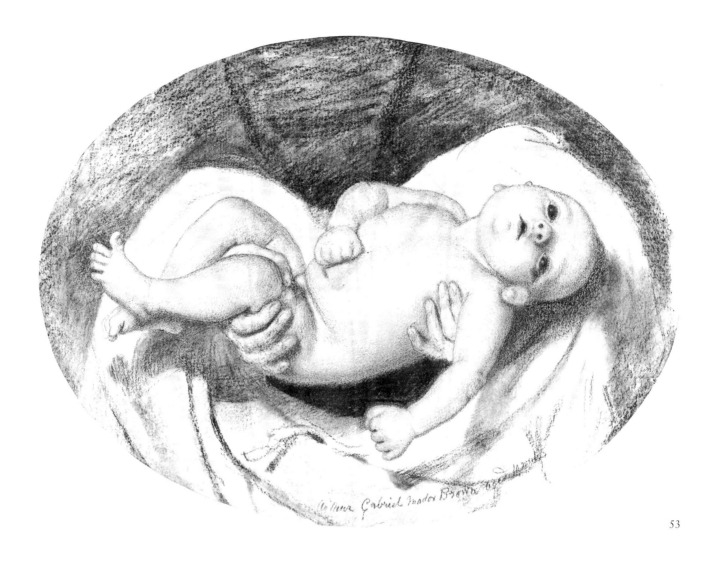

53

53 A Naked Baby held by a Woman

Black chalk and grey wash. 175 × 235 mm (oval)

Inscribed in pencil: *Arthur Gabriel Madox Brown aged 10 weeks*

1894–6–12–7 Purchased from the artist's estate through Messrs Deprez and Gutekunst

Literature: LB 4; Tate Exh., 1984, p. 149; Bennett, Merseyside Colls. Cat., 1988, p. 32

A study for the small unfinished painting in the Tate Gallery, inscribed by the artist with the title *'Take Your Son, Sir'*. The inscription on the drawing dates it towards the end of November 1856, Brown's second son, Arthur, having been born on 16 September.

54

54 'The Prisoner of Chillon'

Pencil. 127 × 95 mm (image)

Signed with monogram in margin lower l. and dated '56

1939–10–14–146 Purchased from Miss J. Wilde, through the
H. L. Florence Fund

Literature: P. Goldman, *Victorian Illustrated Books 1850–
1870* (British Museum 1994), p. 82

A design for the illustration, engraved on wood by the
Dalziel brothers, to the poem by Byron in R. A. Willmott's
anthology *Poets of the Nineteenth Century* (1857). In Paris
in 1842 Brown had painted another, less dramatic, scene
from the same poem, of the three brothers chained to the
pillars in the dungeon.

55

56

55 'The Coat of Many Colours'

Pen and black ink. 199 × 205 mm

Signed with monogram lower r.

1893–10–18–2 Purchased from Dalziel Bros.

Literature: LB 1; Bennett, Merseyside Colls. Cat., 1988, p. 37

A design for the illustration in *Dalziel's Bible Gallery* (1863) of Joseph's brothers showing his bloodstained robe to their father Jacob as proof of his death (Genesis 37). Brown painted a version in oil, dated 1866 (Walker Art Gallery, Liverpool; Tate Exh., 1984, no. 129), and a watercolour dated 1866–7 (Tate).

56 A Man's left Forearm
Verso: Sketch of the upper part of a head

Pencil and grey wash (verso: chalk). 235 × 229 mm

Signed lower l. with monogram and dated 61, and inscribed in brush-point lower r.: *study for Work*

1939–10–14–147 Purchased from Miss J. Wilde through the H. L. Florence Fund

The arm is that of the navvy digging in the centre foreground of the painting *Work* (Manchester Art Gallery), which Brown began in 1852 but did not complete until 1865.

57 Elijah and the Widow's Son

Pencil. 247 × 148 mm

1894–6–12–8 Purchased from the artist's estate through Messrs Deprez and Gutekunst

Literature: LB 3

A design for the illustration in *Dalziel's Bible Gallery* (1863). For the subject see I Kings 17: 17–24. Brown later painted a small-scale version in oil, dated 1864 (Birmingham; Tate Exh., 1984, no. 127) and two in watercolour, one of which is in the Victoria and Albert Museum.

57

Edward Burne Jones
(1833–1898)

In 1853 Edward Jones (he did not use 'Burne' as part of his name until later) went up to Exeter College, Oxford, as a preliminary to taking Holy Orders. There he met a lifelong friend, his fellow-undergraduate William Morris (q.v.), who had had the same intention. They saw and admired Pre-Raphaelite paintings, and soon decided that their future lay in art. In 1856 Jones succeeded in meeting Rossetti, who took him on informally as a pupil, and in the summer of 1857 invited him to take part in the Oxford Union decoration (see no. 17). His earliest independent works (of which the Museum collection has no example) are pen-and-ink drawings in a detailed technique reflecting his study of early German engraving, and in subject-matter and spirit inspired by Rossetti's 'Froissartian' watercolours. In the 1860s he began to paint in watercolour, using, like Rossetti, a combination of watercolour and bodycolour. His first small-scale watercolours still show the influence of Rossetti, but already in the *Chant d'Amour* of 1865 (see no. 62) and *Cupid finding Psyche* of 1866 (no. 58) there is a richness of colour and an amplitude of form that have been described as 'Giorgionesque'. In one sense the term 'Pre-Raphaelite' is more appropriate to him than to Holman Hunt, Millais, Madox Brown and the others: though his point of departure was the romantic mediaevalism of Rossetti, his mature work, however different in total effect, is rich in conscious echoes of Botticelli, Mantegna and other Italian masters of the fifteenth century. He was created a baronet in 1894, when he formally hyphenated his name.

58 Cupid finding Psyche

COLOUR PLATE IV

Watercolour and bodycolour. 668 × 476 mm

Signed lower l. *E. B. J.* and dated *MDCCCLXVI*

Provenance: S. Elliot Lewis (sale, Christie's, 30 November 1934, lot 49); Barbizon House; Cecil French, by whom bequeathed

1954-5-8-8

The composition was originally designed for the illustrated edition of William Morris's *Earthly Paradise* which he and Burne Jones planned in 1865. Burne Jones began with *The*

Story of Cupid and Psyche, and about fifty of his designs were cut on wood, mostly by Morris himself. The project was abandoned in 1868, partly because of the impossibility of finding a modern type-face that could be satisfactorily integrated with the illustrations (it was not until some twenty years later that Morris began the experiments with type design which led to the foundation of the Kelmscott Press); and since *Cupid and Psyche* is only one of twelve sections of *The Earthly Paradise*, the scale of the project may have seem unduly ambitious. Forty-four of the wood-blocks were printed and published in 1974 by Clover Hill Editions, Cambridge.

The present drawing is the earliest of several versions. Another watercolour is in the Manchester Art Gallery and an oil-painting (untraced) was in the collection of F. R. Leyland; another, now in the Birmingham Art Gallery, is one of a series of twelve forming a frieze carried out between 1872 and 1881 in the dining-room of Lord Carlisle's house in Palace Green, Kensington.

59 The Princess Sabra in a Garden

Pencil. 358 × 198 mm

Signed with initials lower r.

Provenance: Sir Edward Poynter, Bt. PRA; sale, Christie's, December 1932, bought through Barbizon House by Cecil French, by whom bequeathed

1954-5-8-9

Literature: Burne-Jones Exh., Arts Council 1975, no. 88

This drawing and nos. 60 and 61 are finished studies for three of the series of seven paintings on canvas illustrating the legend of St George, which Burne Jones painted in 1865–7 for the decoration of The Hill at Witley in Surrey, the house of the landscape watercolourist Myles Birket Foster. The series is now dispersed, and the painting of the princess in the garden is now in the Musée d'Orsay.

60 St George fighting the Dragon

Pencil. 351 × 416 mm

Provenance: as for no. 59

1954–5–8–13

Literature: John Christian, *Art Quarterly*, xxxvi (1973), p. 78; Burne-Jones Exh., Arts Council 1975, no. 89

See no. 59 above. The corresponding painting is in the Art Gallery of New South Wales, Sydney. John Christian has pointed out that the dragon is derived from an early sixteenth-century German wood-cut, attributed to Hans Leinberger, which Burne Jones probably copied in the British Museum.

61 The Return of St George and the Princess

Pencil. 353 × 424 mm

Signed *E. Burne Jones* lower l.

Provenance: as for no. 59

1954–5–8–14

Literature: Burne-Jones Exh., Arts Council 1975, no. 92

See no. 59 above. The corresponding painting is in the Bristol Art Gallery.

62 A kneeling nude Man, holding a Pair of Bellows

Pencil. 289 × 187 mm

Signed with initials lower r., dated *1865*, and inscribed *for LOVE IN THE CHANT D'AMOUR*

Provenance: T. H. Ismay of Dawpool, Cheshire (exhibited BFAC 1899, no. 86); Barbizon House, from where acquired in May 1935 by Cecil French, Burlington Fine Arts Club, by whom bequeathed

1954–5–8–16

The *Chant d'Amour* is a Giorgionesque composition of figures in a landscape, of which there is a watercolour in the Boston Museum and a larger version in oil in the Metropolitan Museum, New York (Tate Exh., 1984, no. 149). A knight in armour is seated on the left, listening to a lady playing on a portable organ, the bellows of which are blown by the kneeling figure of Love. The watercolour was painted in 1865, and the larger version completed in 1877. A note by Cecil French transcribed in the departmental register points out that the date, though inscribed by the artist himself, is incorrect, and that this is a study for the figure in the later version. In the 1865 watercolour the head is at a different angle, and is blindfolded and wearing a wreath of flowers.

According to Burne Jones's own MS record of his work (Fitzwilliam Museum, Cambridge) the larger version was begun in 1868. The date on the drawing must have been added from memory.

60

61

63–69

A group of comic drawings, mostly concerned with William
Morris. They had belonged to Mrs Morris, and then to her
daughter May Morris, and were presented by the latter's
executor Dr Robert Steele.

63 'MR MORRIS reading poems to MR BURNE JONES'

Pen and ink. 92 × 125 mm

Inscribed with title

1939–5–13–12

64 'SED POETA TURPITER SITIENS CANESCIT'

Pen and ink. 169 × 102 mm

Inscribed with title and below: *To J. M. [Jane Morris] from EBJ.
The above will be home about 2 tonight*

1939–5–13–13

63

SED ·POETA TURPITER
SITIONS CANESCIT

TO
J.M.
from
EBJ.

the above will be home about
2 tonight —

64

Grace before meat.

Disgrace after meat

65 Morris Eating

Pen and ink. 37 × 75 mm

1939-5-13-14

66 'Grace before meat Disgrace after meat'

Pen and ink. 150 × 113 mm

Inscribed with title

1939-5-13-15

67 'SOCIETY'

Pen and ink. 130 × 113 mm

Inscribed with title

1939-5-13-26

'SOCIETY.

67

68

68 A Fat Lady looking at the Moon

Pen and ink. 150 × 112mm

1939–5–13–27

THE TIDE! THE TIDE!

69 'THE TIDE! THE TIDE!'

Pen and ink. 152 × 113 mm

Inscribed with title

1939–5–13–28

70 The Annunciation

Watercolour and bodycolour, with touches of gold paint.
522 × 213 mm

Provenance: the Hon. Mrs Percy Wyndham; Cecil French, by whom bequeathed

1954–5–8–15

A small version of the painting, signed and dated 1879, in the Lady Lever Art Gallery, Port Sunlight (Burne Jones Exh., Arts Council 1975, no. 136). Many of Burne Jones's later pictures – for example *The Golden Stairs* (1876–80), *King Cophetua and the Beggar-Maid* (1875–84), *The Depths of the Sea* (1886), and *Danae and the Brazen Tower* (1887–8) – have the same narrow, upright format, which John Christian suggests may have been a consequence of the artist's practice of designing stained glass.

71–73 Three Drawings from *The Flower Book*
'Love in a Tangle'
'Helen's Tears'
'Saturn's Loathing'

Watercolour and bodycolour. 165 mm diameter

Inscribed with titles in pencil upper l. (under mount)

1909–5–12–1 (15, 26, and 31) Purchased from Lady Burne Jones

This series of forty-two small circular watercolours of fanciful compositions inspired by the names of flowers occupied Burne Jones intermittenly from 1882 onwards. After the book was purchased twelve drawings were extracted and mounted separately. In 1905 a facsimile of the book was published by the Fine Art Society.

70

71

72

73

George, Earl of Carlisle
(1843–1911)

74 *The Secret Book of Designs*

Drawings in black chalk, coloured chalks, or watercolour.

1899–7–13–322 to 544   Bequeathed by the artist

Literature: Burne-Jones Exh., Arts Council 1975, no. 327

Burne Jones's monogram is stamped in gold on the red leather cover of this beautifully bound album, containing 222 drawings, carefully inlaid into the album leaves. The drawings date from 1885–9, some relating to projects Burne Jones was working on at the time while others represent ideas too fanciful for development in a more finished form.

75 *Letters to Katie*: Album of Comic Drawings and Illustrated Letters

Pen and ink and pencil.

1960–10–14–2 (1 to 101)   Presented by Miss Katharine Lewis

Literature: Burne-Jones Exh., Arts Council 1975, no. 356

The album contains 101 letters and envelopes, etc., illustrated with comic drawings. They date from the 1880s and are addressed to Katie Lewis, the younger daughter of Burne Jones's friend, the well-known solicitor, Sir George Lewis. The letters, and many of the illustrations, have been published twice, edited by Graham Robertson (1925) and by John Christian (1988).

George Howard, who in 1889 succeeded his uncle as 9th Earl of Carlisle, was associated with the group of English landscape painters working in Italy who called themselves the 'Etruscans', in honour of their master Giovanni Costa; but he was also a friend of many of the Pre-Raphaelite group, especially Burne Jones, and in his watercolours painted directly from nature he could achieve a truly Pre-Raphaelite intensity of observation and mastery of detail. Ruskin himself would have approved the detailed rendering of the cliff-face in the drawing exhibited.

Literature: George Howard and his Circle (Exh. City Art Gallery, Carlisle, 1968)

76 Two Ladies under a Pergola below a Cliff

COLOUR PLATE VI

Watercolour. 365 × 265 mm

1953–10–12–2   Presented by J. A. Gere

No. 55 in the 1968 exhibition at Carlisle is a larger watercolour of a rather similar composition, of a group of Italian peasant-woman under a less elaborate pergola.

Charles Allston Collins

(1828–1873)

Charles Allston Collins was the younger son of William Collins RA, in his day a successful painter of landscape and rustic genre. His elder brother was the novelist Wilkie Collins, and his middle name commemorates his father's friendship with the American painter Washington Allston. As a young man he was a close friend of his fellow-students at the Royal Academy Schools, Holman Hunt and Millais, and a whole-hearted convert to the Pre-Raphaelite doctrine of truth to nature. In the summer of 1850 he and Millais were staying together near Oxford, one working on *Convent Thoughts* (see no. 78), the other on *The Wood-man's Daughter*; and in the summer and autumn of the following year they and Holman Hunt were at Ewell in Surrey, where Hunt began *The Light of the World* and completed *The Hireling Shepherd*, and Millais the background of *Ophelia*. Collins and Millais were also painting backgrounds for as yet undetermined figure-subjects – a characteristic Pre-Raphaelite procedure to which even Rossetti briefly submitted. The methodical and well-organised Millais used his ivy-covered wall for *A Huguenot* (RA 1852), and in 1872 Rossetti transformed the unfinished view in the park at Knole which Hunt had persuaded him to attempt in 1850 into *The Bower Meadow* by the incongruous addition of a group of female figures in his most voluptuous later style; but Collins, having painted the interior of a tumbledown shed, had difficulty in thinking of a suitable subject and left the picture unfinished.

Collins did not share his friends' single-minded dedication to their art. Holman Hunt recalled (*Pre-Raphaelitism*, ii, p. 314) that 'At the time of the vacancy [in the Pre-Raphaelite Brotherhood] occasioned by the retirement of Collinson I judged him to be the strongest candidate as to workmanship, and certainly he could well have held the field for us had he done himself justice in design and possessed courage to keep to his purpose. In his last artistic struggle he continually lost heart when any painting had progressed half-way towards completion, abandoning it for a new subject, and this vacillation he indulged until he had a dozen or more unfinished canvases never to be completed. Of late years he had taken to writing, writing a *New Sentimental Journey* and *A Cruise upon Wheels*'. W. M. Rossetti recorded in *The Pre-Raphaelite Journal* in November 1850

(p. 78) that Collins's election was proposed by Millais, and that Stephens, Hunt and D. G. Rossetti 'acquiesced' – the word implies no very great degree of enthusiasm – but that the proposal was 'savagely' opposed by Woolner, who took the view 'in which I,' wrote W. M. Rossetti, 'fully agree with him, that Collins has not established a claim to P.R.B.-hood, and that the connexion would not be likely to promote the intimate friendly relations necessary between all P.R.B.'s'. Holman Hunt does not refer to Woolner's objection, which seems to have been inspired by some personal antipathy.

Collins exhibited regularly at the Royal Academy from 1849 to 1855, and in 1857 he was represented at the Pre-Raphaelite exhibition at Russell Place by two works, *The Long Engagement* and *The Fuchsia*, both untraced (unless Arthur Hughes's painting with the former title, now in Birmingham, exhibited at the RA in 1859 after he had worked on it for some years, had been sent to the exhibition and catalogued under the wrong name). In 1860 Collins married Charles Dickens's daughter Kate and gave up painting for literature.

The group of eighteen drawings in the Museum collection was bought in 1891, for only £6–6–0, from Charles Fairfax Murray, whose great collection of Pre-Raphaelite drawings was acquired by the Birmingham Art Gallery in 1904. The drawings by Collins had previously belonged to his brother Wilkie, who had died in 1889. They are an important part of his surviving *oeuvre*, which consists otherwise of some half-dozen paintings, the best known being *Convent Thoughts* (see no. 78), which on the whole bear out the contemporary estimate of his talent. A notable exception is *May in the Regent's Park* (dated 1851; exh. RA 1852), acquired by the Tate Gallery only in 1980 and the earliest example of the application of strict Pre-Raphaelite realism to pure landscape. Not surprisingly, the drawings reveal the influence of Millais – indeed, the little drawing of a girl reading a letter (no. 91) could almost be by Millais himself. Apart from the two studies for *Convent Thoughts* they are mostly sketches for unrecorded and presumably unexecuted 'modern subject' compositions, including *The Railway Accident* (nos. 79–82) and '*They that sow in Tears*' (nos. 83–86), both discussed by Alistair Grieve (1976, pp 36ff).

77 Convent Thoughts

Pen and blackish-brown ink. 179 × 108 mm

Provenance: Wilkie Collins; Charles Fairfax Murray (see above)

1891–4–4–12

Literature: LB 1a; Tate Exh., 1984, no. 33

78 Convent Thoughts

Pen and black ink and grey wash over pencil, with some touches of pen and brown ink. 248 × 158 mm

Provenance: as for no. 77

1891–4–4–14

Literature: LB 1b; Tate Exh., 1984, no. 33

The painting, dated 1851, of a young nun in a garden contemplating a passion flower, symbol of the Crucifixion, has been in the Ashmolean Museum, Oxford, since 1894 and is Collins's best-known work. The garden background was painted in the summer of 1850 when he and Millais were staying near Oxford, and the vertical division of the composition by a single standing figure seems to have been inspired by Millais's recently completed *Ferdinand and Ariel* (1849–50). In the two drawings in the British Museum the figure is not wearing a nun's habit, but an ordinary dress. Hunt quotes Millais as saying: 'When [Collins] left Oxford he got hipped about a fancied love-affair, and becoming a High Churchman, changed the subject of his picture from being an illustration of the lady in Shelley's *Sensitive Plant*, who

'. . . out of the cups of the heavy flowers
Emptied the rain of the thunder-showers,

to a picture of a nun' (Hunt, *Pre-Raphaelitism*, i, p. 294). The lady in no. 78 is holding a flower as if pouring water from it.

The 1840s were a period of acute controversy in the Church of England between traditional Protestantism and the Anglo-Catholicism of the Oxford Movement; the Pre-Raphaelite Brotherhood came into existence only three years after the crisis in the Church caused by J. H. Newman's submission to Rome. The staunchly Protestant P.R.B.'s were

anxious that the mediaevalising tendency of their art should not be construed as an expression of High Church sympathies. Hunt urged the substitution of 'Pre-Raphaelite' for Rossetti's 'Early Christian', and even the word 'Brotherhood', was criticised as 'savouring of clericalism'. Collins's devotional fervour must have set him apart from his Pre-Raphaelite associates (Millais found it absurd and teased him about it), and perhaps explains Woolner's opposition to his election.

77

78

79 Study for *The Railway Accident*

Pen and blackish-brown ink, touched with brown wash.
240 × 146 mm

Provenance: as for no. 77

1891–4–4–22

Literature: LB 7b

On the *verso*, a separate study for the head and arm of the little girl in no. 82.

80 Study for *The Railway Accident*

Pen and black ink over pencil sketch, with touches of pen and brown ink and grey wash. 187 × 138 mm

Provenance: as for no. 77

1891–4–4–23

Literature: LB 7a

On the *verso*, a separate study for the lady's head.

81 Study for *The Railway Accident*

Pen and blackish-brown ink, touched with brown wash.
261 × 201 mm

Provenance: as for no. 77

1891–4–4–24

Literature: LB 8b

On the *verso*, a drawing of the head of a bearded man.

82 Study for *The Railway Accident*

Pen and blackish-brown ink, touched with brown wash.
252 × 197 mm

Provenance: as for no. 77

1891–4–4–25

Literature: LB 8a

On the *verso*, a separate study for the lady's head and arm.

The same subject – the title is suggested by Alastair Grieve (p. 37) – is treated in four different ways. A lady wearing a bonnet and veil leans anxiously over the shoulder of a railway telegraph clerk as he slowly takes down a message, letter by letter. That she is married is established by the presence of the little girl in one of the drawings; her husband's train has evidently been involved in an accident and she is concerned for his safety. The point is emphasised by the conspicuous poster reading INSURANCE RAILWAY AC-CIDENT in three of the sketches.

Grieve refers to an unpublished letter from Collins to Hunt, dated 7 February 1855, telling him that the painting is in preparation, along with Millais's *The Rescue* (exh. RA 1855). The latter (National Gallery of Victoria, Melbourne) is another 'modern life' subject involving a domestic disaster, of a fireman carrying two children out of a blazing house. To judge from his drawings, Collins's picture would have had a similarly shaped top.

82

83 Study for '*They that sow in Tears*'

Pen and blackish-brown ink, with brown wash, on pale blue-grey paper. 329 × 203 mm

Provenance: as for no. 77

1891–4–4–26

Literature: LB 9

84 Studies for '*They that sow in Tears*'

Pen and blackish-brown ink, with touches of brown wash, on pale blue-grey paper. 333 × 420 mm

Inscribed: *15*

Provenance: as for no. 77

1891–4–4–27

Literature: LB 10

85 Study for '*They that sow in Tears*'

Pen and blackish-brown ink, with touches of brown wash, over black chalk. 370 × 256 mm

Provenance: as for no. 77

1891–4–4–28

Literature: LB 11

On the *verso* is a rough sketch of a standing figure embracing a kneeling one, as in the composition on no. 89 *verso*, with a third figure standing behind them.

86 Study for '*They that sow in Tears*'

Pen and blackish-brown ink, with brown wash, over black and red chalk. 504 × 313 mm

Provenance: as for no. 77

1891–4–4–29

Literature: LB 12

The title, from Psalm 126, 'They that sow in tears shall reap in joy', is inscribed on no. 83. Grieve suggests (pp. 36ff) that the theme may have been similar to that of *A Magdalen*, a lost early painting which Collins exhibited in 1848, but he admits that the style of the drawings points to a later date, when Collins had come fully under the influence of Millais. In Millais's *The Return of the Dove to the Ark* (1851), *A Huguenot* (1852) and *The Black Brunswicker* (1860) the composition is similarly reduced to a pair of standing figures embracing. Though the female figure in no. 86 is young and pretty enough to fit the conventional pictorial idea of the 'fallen woman', her counterparts in nos. 83 and 84 are elderly and have every appearance of respectability. It seems more likely that the clergyman – a bishop, to judge from his pectoral cross – is consoling a bereaved widow. But the significance of the book in his pocket in no. 83, conspicuously entitled CHURCH MISSION, is obscure.

83

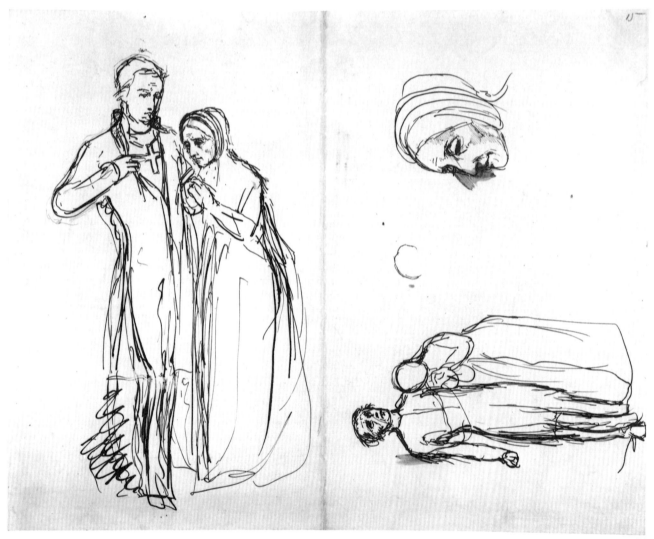

84

85

86

87 A Naval Officer kneeling in Prayer

Pen and blackish-brown ink with touches of brown wash.
260 × 163 mm

Provenance: as for no. 77

1891–4–4–17

Literature: LB 5a

Also on the sheet (which has been trimmed on the right) are
separate sketches of his left shoulder and clasped hands. The
very roughly indicated picture on the wall behind could be a
view, from the sea, of a low building (perhaps a fort) with
hills beyond. See no. 88.

88 verso

88 A Naval Officer kneeling in Prayer, and seated

Pen and blackish-brown ink. 188 × 231 mm

Provenance: as for no. 77

1891–4–4–16

Literature: LB 5b

The epaulettes and sword together with the rings on the
sleeve, show that he is a naval officer. In the sketch on the
right he is seated facing the front, with two positions for his
left arm, one hanging down, presumably over the arm of his
chair, the other raised with the hand holding his forehead.
His facial expression suggests agitation and distress. It has
been drawn over a rapid sketch of the figure kneeling, with
the head bowed between the arms. The scanty surviving
records of Collins's life provide no clue to the subject, but
the style of the drawings is compatible with a date in the
mid-1850s, at the period of the Crimean War.

On the *verso*, a drawing of a young woman holding a
baby.

87

89 Studies for a Painting of a Half-Length Figure of a Little Girl, etc.

Pen and blackish-brown ink with slight indications of pencil sketch on left. 376 × 298 mm

Provenance: as for no. 77

1891–4–4–21

Literature: LB 6

That Collins had a painting in mind is shown by the most complete sketch, in which the composition is enclosed in a frame of the ogival shape favoured by the Pre-Raphaelites and their associates in the 1850s. The child is standing under a tree, clasping a book in her left hand and holding her right forefinger to her mouth in a gesture of indecision. She eyes an apple hanging conspicuously from a bough, and the intended painting can be imagined with some such title as

Temptation. Collins's *The Good Harvest of 1854* (RA 1855; Victoria and Albert Museum; repr. J. Harding, *The Pre-Raphaelites*, 1977, p. 6), of a little girl seen three-quarter length holding a sheaf of corn, may have been the end-product of these studies.

Also on the sheet are two designs for a gothic window, perhaps inspired by the example of Millais, who in 1853 was himself inspired by Ruskin to make a more ingenious and successful design for a window of the same shape, with tracery formed by the wings and sleeves of angels (repr. J.G. Millais, i, p. 204). The man sketched on the upper part of the sheet could be the figure in nos. 87 and 88.

On the *verso* is a rough sketch in pen of a composition with an arched top, inscribed *Passengers by the Ship Augustine.* A man (his dress suggests he may be a clergyman) is seated with an open box or trunk in front of him. Behind him on a table a portrait of a clergyman wearing a stole is propped against a pile of books. On either side are groups of figures embracing. That they are on the deck of a ship is shown by *Notice to Passengers* on the left.

The subject may have to do with the theme of emigration, much in the air in the 1850's. Woolner's departure to seek his fortune in the Australian gold-fields in 1852 inspired Madox Brown's painting *The Last of England.*

90

91

90 An Artist at work, seated, holding a Drawing-Board on his Knees, and two slight Sketches

Pen and blackish-brown ink with touches of wash.
315 × 216mm

Provenance: as for no. 77

1891–4–4–20

Literature: LB 3b

On the *verso* is the lower half of a rough pencil sketch, on a much larger scale, of a lady in a full skirt standing on a terrace bordered by a balustrade.

91 A Lady reading a Letter, in an Interior

Pen and black ink, on head, hair and neck, over pencil.
136 × 136mm

Provenance: as for no. 77.

1891–4–4–13

Literature: LB 3a

93

94

Walter Crane

(1845–1915)

92 A Lady in a wide-brimmed Hat, drawing on a Pair of Gardening-Gloves

Brush drawing in black ink, with touches of watercolour (brown on gloves and hair and green on the fringes of the bodice). 244 × 168 mm

Provenance: as for no. 77

1891–4–4–18

Literature: LB 4a

93 A Lady wearing a wide-brimmed Hat and Gardening-Gloves, holding a Rake in her Right Hand

Brush drawing in black ink over black chalk, with pink wash on the hat-ribbons. 246 × 169 mm

Provenance: as for no. 77

1891–4–4–19

Literature: LB 4b

94 Two Clergymen (?) in Conversation outside a Garden-Gate

Pen and blackish-brown ink. 262 × 373 mm

Provenance: as for no. 77

1891–4–4–15

Literature: LB 2

On the *verso* are sketches of horses and two decorative arrangements of pairs of anchors; also an inscription *My dear Sir* (in ordinary handwriting) *My dear Sir, H. M. S. Justin, 1854*, in small neat script, which might have been intended for a letter to be shown in a painting – possibly the one sketched in nos. 87 and 88. There is no record of any H. M. S. Justin in the Royal Navy.

A leading figure in the Arts and Crafts Movement. Walter Crane is best known for his fanciful and charming illustrations to children's books. In 1871–3 he was in Italy, where he made a number of very beautiful, often rather dark-toned landscape drawings, using a combination of watercolour and bodycolour.

95 A Stream in a Wood

COLOUR PLATE II

Watercolour and bodycolour. 228 × 317 mm

Signed with monogram lower l. and dated *June 25 '74*

1989–9–30–138 Purchased from J. S. Maas

Literature: Victorian Landscape Watercolours (Exh. New Haven, Cleveland, Birmingham, 1992–3), no. 80; Nature in Art Exh., BM 1991, no. 99 (colour repr.).

Painted not long after Crane's return from Italy, and still very much in the spirit of his Italian views. In *An Artist's Reminiscences* (1907) he speaks of his admiration of Burne Jones's 'twilight world of dark mysterious woodlands, haunted streams, meads of deep green starred with burning flowers, veiled in a dim and mystic light'.

Henry Holiday

(1839–1927)

Holiday is now remembered only for two, incongruous, works: the large and at one time much reproduced painting in the Walker Art Gallery, Liverpool, of *Beatrice denying her Salutation to Dante*, and the series of nine fantastic and grotesquely imaginative illustrations to Lewis Carroll's *The Hunting of the Snark* (1876).

At the Royal Academy Schools, where he was a student from 1855 to 1857–8, Holiday was proud to describe himself as 'a Pre-Raphaelite' (see his *Reminiscences of My Life*, 1914). His early work seems to have consisted mostly of landscapes executed in accordance with Pre-Raphaelite principles, and by about 1860 he had made the acquaintance of most of the Pre-Raphaelite circle. His *Burgesses of Calais* of 1858–9 is in the Guildhall Art Gallery, but his *Dante and Beatrice meeting as Children*, of 1859–60, has disappeared. A highly finished drawing of the same subject from the *Vita Nuova* by his close friend and fellow-student Simeon Solomon, inscribed with the date 1859–63, is in the Tate Gallery (Ironside and Gere, fig. 12; Tate Exh., 1984, no. 228). In the 1984 exhibition catalogue, John Christian suggested that Solomon must have been consciously competing with Holiday. Holiday's *The Bride and the Daughters of Jerusalem* (1861–3) has also disappeared, but the study (no. 96) clearly reflects the influence of Rossetti and Burne Jones. By the mid-1860s Holiday was turning increasingly to decorative art, designing stained glass and mural paintings in conjunction with architectural schemes. Twenty years later, the Rossettian subject of *Beatrice denying her Salutation* (1881–3) is in contrast to its correctly academic treatment. In his later years much of his time was devoted to such causes as radical politics and Rational Dress.

96 Two Women in Sixteenth-Century Costume

COLOUR PLATE V

Watercolour and bodycolour. 345 × 203 mm

Provenance: Alfred Holiday (great nephew of the artist), his sale, Christie's, 16 October 1981, lot 72; purchased from John Morton Morris

1982–5–15–22

Literature: Henry Holiday Exh., William Morris Gallery, Walthamstow, 1989, no. 9

A study for two figures in the painting *The Bride and the Daughters of Jerusalem*, begun in 1861 and completed in the following year. The subject is from The Song of Solomon 6: 1. According to the 1989 exhibition catalogue, the picture 'was formerly in the collection of Marlborough College'. Its present whereabouts are unknown, but it is illustrated opposite p. 96 of the artist's *Reminiscences of my Life* (London, 1914).

Arthur Hughes

(1830–1915)

Hughes entered the Royal Academy Schools in 1847, and in 1849 exhibited *Musidora* (Birmingham), a figure-subject in the contemporary academic manner. In 1850 *The Germ* (see no. 38) converted him to Pre-Raphaelitism and he came to know Rossetti, Hunt and Madox Brown. In 1852 he exhibited his first Pre-Raphaelite painting, *Ophelia* (Manchester), and in the same year met Millais, who was to be the chief formative influence on him. In 1857 he painted one of the Arthurian scenes in the Oxford Union (see no. 17). The few slowly-pondered paintings that he produced in the 1850s and early 1860s, especially *April Love* (Exh. 1856, Tate Gallery), *The Long Engagement* (1853–9, Birmingham) and *Home from Sea* (1856–63, Ashmolean Museum, Oxford), are among the most beautiful of all Pre-Raphaelite pictures; but though he continued to paint for the rest of his long life, their level of tension and passion could not be sustained. From the mid-1860s onwards his best work was in book illustration particularly of books for children. These included *At the Back of the North Wind* and others by George Macdonald, Christina Rossetti's *Sing Song* and – rather incongruously for his gentle spirit – *Tom Brown's Schooldays*.

95

97 A Lady standing by a Sundial

Pen and brown ink over pencil. 93 × 56 mm

Inscribed lower r. with monogram *AH*, and below with four lines from Keats's *Isabella*:

Were they unhappy there. It cannot be
    Too many tears for lovers have been shed
Too many sighs give us to them in fee
    Too much of pity after they be dead.

Provenance: the artist (Memorial Exhibition, Walker's Galleries, London, October 1916, no. 80); presented by J. P. Heseltine

1916–11–15–1

On the left her hand is being kissed by a man wearing a helmet of the mid-seventeenth-century 'lobster-tail' pattern worn by cavalrymen in the Civil War. The arched top shows that this must be a sketch for a picture, possibly, as the Memorial Exhibition catalogue claims, *April Love* (Tate

Gallery; exh. RA 1856), the best-known work of Hughes's brief truly Pre-Raphaelite phase, in which a woman is similarly looking away from a man behind her who is kissing her hand. The drawing is dry and diagrammatic by comparison with the fully worked-out pen-and-ink composition study in the Ashmolean Museum, dated April 1857, for the painting *Home from Sea* (Ironside and Gere, pl. 70), but there is nothing about it that seems incompatible with a date in the mid-1850s. It is true that Hughes seems not to have developed his monogram until the mid-1860s, but those on nos. 98, 99 and 100, and on two other drawings which also came from the Memorial Exhibition (*Burlington Magazine*, cxii (1970), p. 454, figs. 33 and 34) all look alike, as if added later and at the same time. (The monogram does not occur on any of the seven illustrations by Hughes in William Allingham's *The Music Master* of 1855.)

The subject of *April Love* is 'modern', but at some stage Hughes may well have considered a seventeenth-century setting and a 'Conflict of Love and Duty' theme involving a

Arthur Hughes

Parliamentarian girl and a Cavalier or *vice versa*, on the lines of Millais's *Huguenot* (1851–2) or, even more, his *The Proscribed Royalist* (1852/3), for which, incidentally, Hughes had been the model. The idea may have been abandoned as being too like *The Proscribed Royalist*, and also W.S.Burton's *A Wounded Cavalier* (Guildhall Art Gallery), exhibited in the 1856 Academy at the same time as *April Love*.

98 Home from Work

Pen and brown ink. 112 × 84 mm

Signed with monogram *AH*

Provenance: as for no. 97 (1916 exh. cat. no. 77); presented by Mrs Francis Dodd

1916–11–15–2

A study for the painting exhibited at the Royal Academy in 1861, now in the Forbes Collection at Battersea House (Ironside and Gere, pl. 66). In the final version the woodman is bending down to embrace the little girl who stands on tiptoe with her arms round his neck, while an older girl wearing a pinafore stands behind her on the threshold of the cottage.

99 'La Belle Dame sans Merci'

Pen and brown ink over pencil. 100 × 59 mm

Inscribed by the artist with title as above, and signed with monogram *AH*

Provenance: as for no. 97 (1916 exh. cat., no. 79); presented by Professor Michael E. Sadler

1916–11–15–3

In his painting of the subject (1862–3), now in the National Gallery of Victoria in Melbourne, the knight stands looking up at the lady, who is mounted on his horse; in a sketch in the Carlisle Art Gallery both figures are on horseback, the knight embracing the lady (both repr. Robin Gibson, 'Arthur Hughes: Arthurian and related subjects of the early 1860s' in *Burlington Magazine* cxii (1970), p. 454).

A watercolour by Rossetti dated 1855, of a man walking arm in arm with a young woman who holds an apple (S 76),

98

has always been called 'La Belle Dame sans Merci' (see no. 16), but critics have observed that it has no obvious connexion with Keats's poem. The man is not wearing armour, and though his costume is mediaeval its only knightly feature is the spurs on his boots. Rossetti himself referred to it as 'that drawing of mine with a music note in the corner' (i.e. a treble clef followed by the notes G and D, the significance of which has never been explained); and Ruskin, who owned it, as 'that man with boots and lady with golden hair' and 'The Man and his Blue Wife'. Fairfax Murray thought the figures might be Laertes and Ophelia. But the fact that Hughes was contemplating a treatment of the subject with the two figures standing, and without the horse, suggests that the traditional interpretation of Rossetti's drawing may be correct.

126

99

100

William Henry Millais

(1828–1899)

The little that is known of Millais's elder brother is gleaned from incidental references in J. G. Millais's life of his father. In the early 1850s the two brothers were much together: William was one of the party at Ewell in the summer of 1851, along with his brother, Holman Hunt and Charles Collins, and two years later accompanied his brother to Scotland. In his account of the Millais household at the time when he was acting as model for *The Proscribed Royalist* (J. G. Millais, i. pp. 172 ff.), Arthur Hughes refers to William Millais's 'picturesque but somewhat restless individuality', and adds that 'his forte was watercolour landscapes, exquisitely drawn' – a judgement confirmed by the present drawing. He exhibited landscapes in the Royal Academy in 1852–3, 1876, and in 1890–3.

101 A Scottish Farmstead

COLOUR PLATE III

Watercolour. 180 × 329 mm

Signed: *W H Millais*

1974–6–15–8 Purchased from J. S. Maas

Literature: British Landscape Watercolours Exh., BM 1985, no. 190

100 'La Belle Dame sans Merci'

Pen and brown ink. 83 × 91 mm

Inscribed by the artist with monogram *AH*

Provenance: as for no. 97

1916–11–15–4

See no. 99.

William Morris

(1834–1896)

After coming down from Oxford in 1856 Morris went into the office of the Gothic Revival architect G. E. Street with the intention of making architecture his profession. At about the same time he and Burne Jones had come to know Rossetti, whose dictum that 'the man who has any poetry in him ought to paint it; the next Keats ought to be a painter' persuaded him to give up architecture for painting, but his career as a painter was brief. In June 1857 Rossetti wrote to William Bell Scott 'Morris has as yet done nothing in art, but is now busily painting his first picture, *Sir Tristram after his Illness in the Garden of King Mark's Palace, recognised by the Dog he had given to Iseult*, from the *Morte d'Arthur*. It is being done all from nature of course, and I believe will turn out capitally'. In the same year a watercolour is recorded of '"The Soldan's Daughter in the Palace of Glass" . . . seated in a heavy wooden armchair, probably studied from one of those at Red Lion Square, and the palace was in all shades of bluish glass'. Both have disappeared, and the only easel-painting by Morris now known is the *Queen Guenevere* painted in Oxford in 1858, for which no. 102 is probably a study. In the summer of 1857 Morris had been enlisted by Rossetti to help decorate the Oxford Union (see no. 17). Though his 'fresco' of a scene from the *Morte d' Arthur* was a failure, the formal pattern which he devised for the ceiling of the room was the most successful part of the entire scheme and showed that his true bent lay in pattern-making and in decorative and applied art.

Morris's father had been a prosperous stockbroker, and he enjoyed the luxury of an independent income. This enabled him, while still an undergraduate, to buy Arthur Hughes's *April Love* and Madox Brown's *The Hayfield* (both now Tate Gallery), and later to subsidise the 'Firm' until it began to show a profit. More immediately, after his marriage to Jane Burden in 1859, he could begin to build the Red House at Bexley, in Kent, to the design of Philip Webb, a friend made in Street's office. The commercially produced furniture of the period did not suit the austerely mediaeval style of Webb's interior. Morris himself had devised 'intensely mediaeval tables and chairs, like incubi and succibi', as Rossetti described them, for the rooms which he and Burne Jones shared in Red Lion Square, and he now asked Webb to design the furniture for the new house. This led to the foundation in 1861 of Morris, Marshall, Faulkner & Co. (see no. 32), in which Webb, Rossetti, Madox Brown and Burne Jones were also partners, dedicated to the improvement of domestic and ecclesiastical furniture and decoration. In the last quarter of the nineteenth century the influence of the 'Firm' was enormous, especially for the wallpapers and fabrics which Morris himself designed. In his later years Morris became interested in printing and book design, and in 1890 founded the Kelmscott Press.

After 1874 Rossetti and Morris ceased to see one another (see no. 32), but Burne Jones remained a close friend. Both were fascinated by his genius and, as their caricatures of him show (nos. 25–32, 63–66), by the egocentric vehemence of his personality. The word 'genius' is justified by his instinctive and immediate mastery of every means of artistic expression. His poems, especially in his earliest volume, *The Defence of Guenevere* (1858), some of which are inspired by Rossetti's 'Arthurian' watercolours, establish him as a minor classic; and though his first attempt at painting on an unfamiliarly large scale was a failure, the *Queen Guenevere*, also of 1858, is a remarkably accomplished work for a novice. Eventually he came to regard easel-painting as a dead end: painting for him was part of a decorative scheme, its proper place either on walls or on furniture.

102 Head of Jane Burden (Mrs Morris)

Pen and black ink and grey wash. 104 × 76 mm (a horizontal fold in the centre of the sheet)

Provenance: Mrs Morris; her daughter, Jane Morris; presented by the latter's executor, Dr Robert Steele

1939–6–2–1

In the late summer of 1857 Rossetti and Burne Jones, then in Oxford engaged on the decoration of the Union (see no. 17), went one evening to the theatre, where they were struck by the extraordinary beauty of a girl in the audience. They succeeded in making her acquaintance, and in persuading her to act as a model for their paintings. She appears as Guenevere in Rossetti's *Sir Lancelot's Vision of the Sanc Grail* in the Union, and in Morris's only known easel-picture, the *Queen Guenevere* (also sometimes known as *La*

John William North

(1841–1924)

Belle Iseult) which he painted in 1858 (Tate Gallery), and for which the present drawing may be a preliminary study. He is said to have scrawled on the canvas 'I cannot paint you, but I love you'; and in April 1859 they were married.

By the late 1850s Rossetti's relationship with Elizabeth Siddal was under increasing strain, and he too was attracted by Jane Burden. She, for her part, found Morris a not altogether congenial husband, and a triangular relationship gradually developed in which he seems to have been the odd man out. Mrs Morris, who behaved with impeccable dignity and discretion, became Rossetti's confidante and intimate friend, as well as his chief source of artistic inspiration and his favourite model. Her face haunts his paintings from the late 1860s onwards, as Elizabeth Siddal's does those of the 1850s. The letters they exchanged (more of his than hers seem to have survived) from 1868 until 1881 – the year before Rossetti's death – were published in 1976 by John Bryson in association with Janet Camp Troxell. Jane Morris herself died in 1914.

The 'Idyllists' was the term used to describe North and his friends Fred Walker (q.v.), George John Pinwell and, after his return from Italy, George Hemming Mason, with their particular style of rustic genre. Much of North's best work was in the form of book illustration (see Forrest Reid, *Illustrators of the Eighteen Sixties*, 1928, pp. 163 etc.).

103 Halsway Court, Somerset

COLOUR PLATE III

Watercolour and bodycolour. 330 × 445 mm

Signed lower l. with initial *N* and dated '65

1994-7-23-2 Purchased from Robin de Beaumont, with a contribution from the National Art Collections Fund

Literature: Christopher Newall, *Victorian Watercolours*, 1987, pp. 84–8; *Victorianische Malerei*, British Council Exh., Neue Pinakothek, Munich and Prado, Madrid, 1993, no. 87

This picturesque and romantic fifteenth-century house in the Quantock Hills in Somerset was taken by North on more than one occasion, and often appears in his watercolours and book-illustrations. This drawing is a particularly fine example of his watercolour technique.

102

John Ruskin
(1819–1900)

Frederick Sandys
(1829–1904)

Ruskin's role in the Pre-Raphaelite Movement was as champion and defender in its early stages, and as practical supporter and patron especially of Rossetti and Millais. His father collected landscape watercolours of the contemporary English school, and John Ruskin's first attempts at drawing are in the 'picturesque' style of David Roberts, Prout, Copley Fielding and Turner. His later drawings, from about 1845, are of architectural details, clouds, landscapes, flowers, trees, shells, rocks (a passionate geologist, he collected minerals with the same enthusiasm as he did mediaeval manuscripts or watercolours by Turner), in short, of almost every natural phenomenon except the human figure. He made no attempt at composition or selection. As he once wrote, 'I have no power of design, I can only paint what I see'. Given this limitation, his drawings are unsurpassed for delicacy of touch and an exquisite precision and sensitiveness of eye and hand.

104 A Rock covered with Ivy and Lichen

COLOUR PLATE VII

Watercolour with touches of bodycolour. 400 × 270 mm (image), 455 × 346 mm (sheet)

Inscribed on verso: *Study of ivy – Coniston*

1979–1–27–11 Purchased from the Maas Gallery

Literature: Andrew Wilton and Anne Lyles, *The Great Age of British Watercolours 1750–1880* (Exh. Royal Academy and National Gallery, Washington, 1993), no. 247 (Section III)

Ruskin had a particular feeling for ivy. In his autobiography, *Praeterita*, he recalled how in May 1842, 'one day on the road to Norwood, I noticed a bit of ivy round a thorn stem, which seemed, even to my critical judgment, not ill "composed"; and proceeded to make a light and shade pencil study of it in my grey paper pocket book, carefully, as if it had been a bit of sculpture, liking it more and more as I drew. When it was done, I saw that I had virtually lost all my time since I was twelve years old, because no one had ever told me to draw what was really there! All my time, I mean, given to a drawing as an art; I had never seen the beauty of anything, not even of a stone – much less of a leaf.' The present drawing must date from at least thirty years later: Ruskin moved to his house on Coniston Water in 1872.

In 1857 Sandys published the well-known 'zinco-engraving' entitled *A Nightmare*, which parodied Millais's painting *Sir Isumbras at the Ford*, exhibited at the RA in that year and savagely criticised by Ruskin. It showed Ruskin as a braying ass ridden by Millais, with Hunt and Rossetti as the two children whom the old knight in the painting is carrying across the ford (see *Burlington Magazine*, cvii (1965), p. 251).

Sandys had made Rossetti's acquaintance when he called on him in order to study his appearance at first hand. The satire appealed to his sense of humour, and a friendship developed. After the death of Rossetti's wife in 1862 Sandys became one of his intimate circle, but offended by rumours that Rossetti was accusing him of artistic plagiarism he broke off relations in 1869. His paintings of idealised half-length female figures are unquestionably Rossettian (*Medea*, painted in 1866–8 and now in the Birmingham Art Gallery, is an example), but they are the least important part of his work. Sandys was above all a draughtsman of exceptional originality and skill, at his best in the designs for wood-engraved illustrations which he made in the 1860s for magazines like *Good Words* and *Once a Week*, and which reflect the influence of the contemporary German school of illustrators such as Alfred Rethel and Julius Schnorr (see Forrest Reid, *Illustrators of the Eighteen Sixties*, 1928, pp. 55 etc. and Paul Goldman, *Victorian Illustrated Books*, 1850–1870, 1994, pp. 97 etc.). In the 1870s he developed an individual style of carefully finished portrait drawing using coloured chalks on tinted paper, but the drawing exhibited must have been made in 1858–9 when Ruth Herbert was one of Rossetti's favourite models, and is entirely in his manner.

105 Ruth Herbert

Black chalk with touches of white chalk on pale brown paper. 409 × 160 mm

Signed lower l. with monogram

1910–10–13–25 Purchased from Mrs Frederick Sandys

As an actress Louisa Ruth Herbert called herself Louisa Herbert. Rossetti, who first met her in 1858 and addressed her as 'loveliest of your sex and goddess of the P.R.B.', always refers to her as Ruth Herbert. In 1858–9 she was one of his favourite models, and he drew and painted many portraits of her (S 325–336). It was for her that he painted the watercolour *Writing on the Sand* (no. 20) in 1859, and the drawing of her by Sandys must date from about the same time.

105

William Bell Scott

(1811–1890)

Like Rossetti, though on a very much lesser scale, Scott was both poet and painter. A younger brother, and eventually the biographer, of the remarkable romantic painter David Scott (1806–49), he was born and trained in Edinburgh. When David Scott took part in the competition for the decoration of the Houses of Parliament in 1843 his brother became known to the official world, and in 1844 was put in charge of the newly established Government School of Design in Newcastle upon Tyne. Scott was an intimate and faithful friend of Rossetti, who had written to him in 1847 expressing admiration of his poems. He was also a friend of Holman Hunt, and contributed two poems to *The Germ* in 1850; but he remained in Newcastle until 1864, which prevented him from any close involvement in the affairs of the Pre-Raphaelite circle. His verse is unmemorable. Of his paintings the best known are the scenes from the history of Northumberland at Wallington Hall (especially the last, *Iron and Coal*: Ironside and Gere, pls. 1–3), begun in 1856, and those illustrating the poem *The King's Quair*, painted in 1865–8 on the wall of the staircase of his friend Alice Boyd's Penkill Castle (see no. 106). He is now chiefly remembered for Max Beerbohm's drawing of him 'wondering what it is those fellows seem to see in Gabriel' (*Rossetti and his Circle*, pl. 14), which reflects the not entirely just impression that the candid account of Rossetti's foibles in his two volumes of amusing and informative *Autobiographical Notes*, published posthumously in 1892, was inspired by disgruntled jealousy.

106 Interior with a Man and a Woman embracing on a Sofa

Brush drawing in brown, pale reddish-brown and black wash, with touches of white bodycolour. 124 × 172 mm

Signed lower r. with monogram, and dated *19 July 1863*

1974–6–15–7 Purchased from the Langton Gallery

The unusually large and conspicuously inscribed date may have some significance: it is tempting to wonder whether the drawing commemorates some crisis in the relationship of Scott and his pupil, devoted friend and constant companion, Alice Boyd of Penkill Castle in Ayrshire. The woman on the sofa could well be her, to judge from a portrait drawing by Scott dated July 1861, formerly at Penkill (house sale, Christie's, 15 December 1992, lot 145, repr.)

They met in Newcastle in March 1859, when he was forty-eight, a talented artist and poet and unhappily married, and she thirty-four, attractive but unmarried and looking for someone to help her develop her skill as an artist. Not surprisingly, they fell in love. After Scott and his wife moved to London in 1864, a successful *ménage à trois* was established. The Scotts spent the summers at Penkill, and Miss Boyd lived with them in London in the winter. Mrs Scott accepted the fact of her husband's liaison. The two women remained, at least outwardly, on good terms, and no-one questioned the propriety of the arrangement. Scott and Alice Boyd remained a devoted couple until his death in 1890. She died in 1897.

107 King Edward's Bay

COLOUR PLATE VI

Watercolour, with some white bodycolour. 251 × 353 mm

Provenance: Jacob Burnett, of Collingwood House, Tynemouth (according to label formerly on frame: for Burnett, 1825–1896, see Laing Art Gallery cat., p. 126); presented by J. A. Gere

1954–3–2–1

Literature: British Landscape Watercolours Exh., BM 1985, no. 178, pl. 126; *Pre-Raphaelites: Painters and Patrons in the North-East* (Exh. Laing Art Gallery, Newcastle-upon-Tyne, 1989–90), no. 108

The title was inscribed on an old label. King Edward's Bay is near Tynemouth. Scott was based in Newcastle upon Tyne from 1845 to 1864.

106

Arthur Severn
(1842–1931)

He was the younger son of the painter Joseph Severn, now best remembered as having been with Keats in Rome when the poet died in 1820. He exhibited landscape watercolours, and has been described as 'essentially a water, sun and sky painter'. In 1871 he married Joan Agnew, a cousin of the Ruskins, who had acted as companion to Ruskin's mother, who died in that year. When Ruskin then moved from Denmark Hill, in South London, to the Lake District, the Severns accompanied him and remained part of the household until his death. Arthur Severn's recollections of Ruskin, edited by James Dearden, were published in 1967 under the title *The Professor*.

108 Gordale Scar

Watercolour and bodycolour. 246 × 352 mm

Signed and dated: *A. Severn 1877*

1988–4–9–3 Purchased from Oscar and Peter Johnson Ltd.

108

Elizabeth Eleanor Siddal

(1834–1862)

Walter Deverell was responsible for introducing Elizabeth Siddal to the Pre-Raphaelite circle. Struck by the extraordinary beauty of the twenty-year-old assistant in a bonnet-shop, he persuaded his mother to approach her and ask if she would consider posing as a model. Elizabeth Siddal was the model for Viola in his *Twelfth Night* (1850), for a figure in Holman Hunt's *Converted British Family sheltering a Christian Priest* (1850) and for Sylvia in his *Valentine rescuing Sylvia from Proteus* (1851: see no. 1), as well as for Millais's *Ophelia* (1852); but from then onwards Rossetti monopolised her attention, and for the next ten years she was his constant companion and source of inspiration, and finally, briefly his wife.

Her brother-in-law W. M. Rossetti described her as 'tall, with a stately throat and fine carriage, a pink and white complexion, and massive, straight, coppery-golden hair. Her large greenish-blue eyes, large-lidded, were particularly noticeable'. Lady Burne Jones remembered 'the mass of her beautiful deep-red hair as she took off her bonnet . . . Her complexion looked as if a rose tint lay beneath the white skin, producing a most soft and delicate pink for the darkest flesh tone. Her eyes were of a kind of golden brown – agate colour is the only word I can find to describe them – and wonderfully luminous . . . The eyelids were deep, but without any langour or drowsiness, and had the peculiarity of seeming scarcely to veil the light in her eyes when she was looking down'. Swinburne, who was devoted to her, wrote of her 'deep-gold hair and luminous grey-green eyes shot through with colours of sea-water in sunlight, and threaded with faint keen lines of fire and light about the pupil'. A dissenting voice comes from another poet and friend of Rossetti, William Allingham, who found 'her pale face, abundant red hair, and long thin limbs . . . strange and affecting' rather than beautiful.

The lives and personalities of the Pre-Raphaelite group, and especially Rossetti's, have been the subject of intense and sometimes sensation-mongering scrutiny; but unconventional though his relationship with Miss Siddal was, no one has ever suggested that she was his mistress. It was understood that he would eventually marry her and they were treated as an engaged couple, but his impecunious and disordered way of life was not conducive to matrimony. As passion faded and her health declined their relationship came under increasing strain. Finally, in May 1860, he married her; a year later she gave birth to a still-born child; and in February 1862 she died of an overdose of laudanum. Her death was certainly deliberate: according to Helen Angeli, who as William Rossetti's daughter and Madox Brown's granddaughter was in a position to know the truth, a slip of paper pinned to her nightgown bore the message 'Take care of Harry' – her feeble-minded brother to whom she was devoted. Overcome by grief and remorse, Rossetti insisted on putting in her coffin the only complete manuscript of his own poems: an impulsive gesture which he came to regret seven years later, when the grave had to be opened to recover the book.

It is impossible to form any positive idea of Elizabeth Siddal's personality. Her drawings, though inevitably derivative from her husband, and her verses, equally derivative from him and his sister Christina, have a flavour of their own, if in a minor key (Forrest Reid, in his *Illustrators of the Eighteen Sixties*, is surely unjust in seeing in her drawings nothing but 'a yearning mawkishness'); but in none of the by now considerable number of published Pre-Raphaelite reminiscences and documents is she recorded as expressing an opinion, or indeed as saying anything at all. Nevertheless, the Pre-Raphaelite world of the 1850s is haunted by her withdrawn, elusive presence – 'a shadow like an angel, with bright hair'.

109a. Roundel of an Angel holding Cymbals
109b. A Woman with Arms outstretched looking out of a Window

a. Pencil. b. Pen and brown wash over pencil, On the l. and r. halves of a sheet of folded notepaper stamped 'Extra Satin'. 180 × 229 mm

Provenance: Presented by Dr Robert Steele (see no. 25)

1941–9–1–1

Literature: S 699

109

110

111

110a. Sketch of a Figure turned to the left with another Figure behind
110b. Roundel of an Angel holding Cymbals

a. Pencil. b. Pen and brown wash. On the l. and r. halves of a sheet of folded notepaper, stamped 'Partridge and Cozens Ivory'. 180 × 227 mm

Inscribed in pen: *Sept 9th*

Provenance: as for no. 109

1941−9−1−2

Literature: S 699A

111 Sketch of an Angel holding Cymbals

Pencil. On a half sheet of notepaper, with the same stamp as on no. 109. 180 × 115 mm

Provenance: as for no. 109

1941−9−1−3

Literature: S 699B

A modern hand (Dr Steele's?) has inscribed in pencil below no. 109b *?Mrs Rossetti* and below no. 110b *?Rossetti*. Virginia Surtees followed this distinction, attributing no. 109b to Elizabeth Siddal and the others to Rossetti himself. But in style and handling the group is surely homogeneous, and Rossetti's authorship of the roundel designs can surely be ruled out on grounds of quality. Furthermore, a photograph of a sketch for the same roundel, containing three cymbal-bearing angels preceded by three doves (a single dove is indicated in nos. 110b and 111) is on p. 14 of the album in the Fitzwilliam Museum, Cambridge, inscribed in Rossetti's hand on the first leaf: *Photographs from designs and sketches by Elizabeth Eleanor Rossetti given to Charles A. Howell by his friend D.G. Rossetti 18th January 1867.*

On p. 9 of the Fitzwilliam album is a photograph of a drawing of a woman looking out of a window as in no. 109b, but with her arms outstretched to the right, inscribed by Rossetti *Tennyson St Agnes*. In the Moxon *Tennyson* of 1857 a drawing by Millais of a woman standing on a spiral staircase, looking through an open window down to a snow-covered courtyard, illustrates the opening lines of the poem *St Agnes Eve*:

Deep on the convent roof the snows
  Are sparkling to the moon:
My breath to heaven like vapour goes:
  May my soul follow soon!

Though in no. 109b the snow-covered roofs are not shown, as they are in the photographed drawing, this could be interpreted as a variant of the same subject were it not for the object in the left foreground, which seems to be an embroidery frame. If so, the drawing probably illustrates another poem by Tennyson, *The Lady of Shalot*, who

. . . weaves by night and day
A magic web with colours gay.
She has heard a whisper say,
A curse is on her if she stay
  To look down to Camelot,

showing her at the moment when she disregards the curse and looks out of the window. Rossetti and Elizabeth Siddal would have discussed the project for the illustrated Tennyson: she was the 'certain young lady' who should have been asked to collaborate (see no. 2).

James Smetham
(1821–1889)

Smetham was a curiously isolated figure, conscious of his own isolation. In 1854 he told Ruskin: 'I have felt the dearth of intercourse on the subject of my occupations . . . With artists generally I have not felt much drawn to associate' (*Letters*, 1902, p. 8). The son of a Wesleyan minister and a lifelong member of the sect, he evolved 'a plan of life, beginning in a course of long disciplinary study, and intended to combine art, literature, and the religious life all in one'. At first he supported himself by painting small-scale portraits; when photography began to supersede this means of livelihood, he became drawing-master at the Wesleyan Normal College in Westminster. He achieved no popular success, and for the last twelve years of his life was afflicted with madness brought on by a combination of religious melancholia and a sense of disappointment and failure. His work was admired and encouraged by Ruskin, and by Rossetti who remained a faithful friend, and whose letters show that as late as 1878 he was concerned for his well-being.

In 1869 Rossetti described Smetham, apropos of his long review of Gilchrist's *Life of Blake*, reprinted in the second edition, as: 'a painter and designer of our own day who is, in many signal respects, very closely akin to Blake; more so probably than any other living artist could be said to be. James Smetham's work – generally of small or moderate size – ranges from Gospel subjects, of the subtlest imaginative and mental insight, and sometimes of the grandest colouring, through Old Testament compositions and through poetic and pastoral of every kind to a special imaginative form of landscape.

'In all these he partakes greatly of Blake's immediate spirit, being also often nearly allied by landscape intensity to Samuel Palmer, in his youth the noble disciple of Blake. Mr Smetham's works are very numerous, and, as other exclusive things have come to be, will some day be known in a wide circle.'

Copies of two MS lists of Smethan's works are in the Department of Prints and Drawings.

112 'The Knight's Bridal'

COLOUR PLATE I

Watercolour. 289 × 253 mm

Provenance: F. Stead? (see below); purchased from the Fine Art Society

1977–4–2–3

Presumably to be identified with the watercolour entitled 'The Knight's Bridal' included in both lists of the artist's works under the date 1865, purchased for 10 guineas by a Mr F. Stead; the dimensions given, 15 by 12 inches, are greater than those of the British Museum drawing (11⅜ by 10), but the discrepancy does not seem enough to invalidate the identification. An oil-painting of the same size, entitled 'The Knight's Vow', is listed immediately afterwards.

In the later 1850s Smetham's technique was temporarily influenced by Pre-Raphaelite realism (as in his *Naboth's Vineyard* of 1856, in the Tate Gallery). 'The Knight's Bridal' is clearly inspired by Rossetti's 'chivalric' watercolours, Smetham's enthusiasm for which is shown by his often-quoted description of *The Marriage of St George* as: 'a golden, dim dream. Love "credulous all gold", gold armour, a sense of secret enclosure in "palace chambers far apart"; but quaint chambers in quaint palaces where angels creep in through sliding panel doors, and stand behind rows of flowers, drumming on golden bells, with wings crimson and green'.

Simeon Solomon

(1840–1905)

Simeon Solomon forms a link between Pre-Raphaelitism and the 'Aesthetic' and 'Decadent' movements of the later nineteenth century. His family were orthodox Jews, and among his early works, foreshadowing his later fascination with ritual and hieratic ceremonial, was a series of illustrations of Jewish religious rites in present-day settings (*Once a Week*, 1862). By about 1860 he had become one of the Pre-Raphaelite circle. Drawings like *Dante's First Meeting with Beatrice*, dated 1859–63 (Tate Gallery; Tate Exh., 1984, no. 228), and *The Painter's Pleasaunce*, datable *c*.1861–2 (see no. 115), were inspired by Rossetti in subject and treatment, but the titles of his exhibits at the Royal Academy between 1858 and 1864 show that at first his preferred subjects were from the Old Testament (cf. nos. 113, 114) or of Jewish ceremonial. In 1872 the painting '*Habet!*', of Roman ladies watching a gladiatorial combat, marks the beginning of a shift of interest towards classical history and mythology, encouraged by his friendship with the poet Swinburne. Other influences on his later style were the androgynous sentiment of such Italian Renaissance masters as Leonardo da Vinci and his followers Boltraffio and Luini, and the contemporary French 'Symbolist' school of Gustave Moreau (see no. 116). In 1871 he published a long, rhapsodic prose poem *A Vision of Love Revealed in Sleep*, in a style perhaps inspired by another literary friend, Walter Pater. It was reviewed by Swinburne, who wrote: 'I have heard him likened to Heine as a kindred Hellenist of the Hebrews; Grecian form and beauty divide the allegiance of his spirit with Hebrew shadow and majesty'.

In 1873 Solomon was convicted of a homosexual offence, with the result that he became a 'non-person'. For more than thirty years, unrepentant and incorrigible, he led a jovial, drunken existence on the fringe of the London underworld, sometimes earning a few shillings as a pavement artist or by turning out perfunctory drawings of idealised androgynous heads in red chalk. Had he not fallen from grace in the way he did, there would inevitably have been a full-scale biography enriched with reminiscences and information from his friends. Given the wide range of his contacts in artistic and literary circles, this would have been a valuable addition to Pre-Raphaelite literature; as it is, the few references to him in memoirs and letters are brief and embarrassed.

113

113 A Kneeling Bearded Man

Brown wash over pencil. 90 × 102 mm

Inscribed by the artist: *ISAIAH*

Provenance: Hollyer Family; Cecil French, by whom bequeathed

1954–5–8–20

Inscribed by Cecil French, on a label detached from the former frame: *From the Hollyer Family. The Purification of Isaiah, about 1860*.

114

114 A Nude Youth and an Old Man

Pen and brown wash, over pencil. 230 × 105 mm

Inscribed in ink: *61 Paris*, and in pencil close to trimmed r. edge *Study for an . . . in Worship of . . . figure of Old man*, and below the figures *Angel* and *Ezekiel*.

Provenance: Robert Ross; Cecil French, by whom bequeathed

1954–5–8–19

Inscribed by Cecil French, on a label detached from the former frame: *Study for Ezekiel and the Angel 1861. Formerly in the possession of Robert Ross.*

115 The Painter's Pleasaunce

Watercolour. 120 × 133 mm

Signed lower l. with initial *S*

Provenance: Purchased at Leicester Galleries, April 1932, by Cecil French, by whom bequeathed

1954–5–8–17

A larger version, also in watercolour, is dated 2 December 1861 (Whitworth Gallery, Manchester; Tate Exh., 1984, no. 233, where John Christian refers to the mid-nineteenth-century vogue in France and England for subjects drawn from the lives of Renaissance painters). Between *c.*1852 and 1857 Rossetti produced four different compositions of such painters engaged on portraits (S 54, 89, 694, 695), in the last of which a bearded young man is painting a richly dressed young lady seated in a chair. He is clearly meant to be Giorgione, who is probably also the artist in Solomon's drawing, as Christian suggests.

The British Museum version corresponds with the other in all essentials and has the appearance of a small-scale autograph replica, such as the Pre-Raphaelites often made, rather than a preliminary study.

116 Amoris Sacramentum

Pencil with some outlines gone over in black ink, and with watercolour on the right sleeve and 'monstrance' and on the head. 335 × 200 mm

1922–4–8–1 Presented by C. H. V. Bancalari

Literature: Solomon: a Family of Painters (Exh. Geffrye Museum, London, and Birmingham, 1985/6), no. 60

The drawing corresponds closely with a painting said to have belonged to Oscar Wilde, now lost but known from the plate in Percy Bate's *English Pre-Raphaelite Painters* (1899), opp. p. 66, on which are superimposed in white Solomon's monogram and the date 1868, no doubt illegible in the photograph. In the drawing the figure holds in his left hand a staff from which spring budding branches; in the painting this has become a *thyrsus* – the pine-cone-tipped rod which was one of the attributes of Bacchus. The object held in the right hand seems to be a profane

115

variation of a monstrance, the vessel used by a priest to display the Host.

The hieratic impassivity of the figure and the highly-wrought jewelled regalia of mysterious or ambiguous significance are paralleled in the paintings which the French 'Symbolist' Gustave Moreau was exhibiting from about 1865 onwards. Moreau's work, and possibly even Moreau himself, must have been known to Solomon. No. 114 is inscribed *61 Paris*, but no information about his contacts in France seems to have survived. The parallel between Moreau and Burne Jones was discussed by Robin Ironside (*Horizon*, June 1940; reprinted *Apollo*, March 1975).

Fred Walker

(1840–1875)

Like his friend J. W. North (q.v.), Walker was one of the 'Idyllist' group, and like North much of his work was done for book illustration (see Forrest Reid, *Illustrators of the Eighteen Sixties*, 1928, pp. 134 etc.).

117 An Amateur

Watercolour and bodycolour. 177 × 253 mm

Provenance: Cecil French, by whom bequeathed

1954–5–8–21

Literature: British Landscape Watercolours Exh., BM 1985, no. 194; *Viktorianische Malerei*, British Council Exh., Neue Pinakothek, Munich and Prado, Madrid, 1993, no. 89

117

Appendix

A complete list of all drawings and watercolours in the Department of Prints and Drawings of the British Museum by the artists included in the exhibition.

Artists are listed in alphabetical order and the works of each are listed roughly in chronological order. References are given to the following catalogues:

G
The present catalogue

LB
Laurence Binyon, *Catalogue of Drawings by British Artists in the Department of Prints and Drawings in the British Museum*, 4 vols. (1898–1907)

S
Virginia Surtees, *The Paintings and Drawings of Dante Gabriel Rossetti*, 2 vols. (Oxford, 1971)

St
Lindsay Stainton, *British Landscape Watercolours 1600–1860* (Exh. BM, 1985)

George Price Boyce
(1826–1897)

Bettwys-y-Coed in the evening, 1851
Watercolour, on buff paper. 154 × 278 mm
1970–10–31–7

San Giorgio Maggiore from the Piazzetta, Venice – Moonlight Study, 1854
Watercolour, in artist's mount and frame. 187 × 280 mm (sight)
1994–5–14–29 Presented by Mrs Anne E. Christopherson

A Farmhouse at Streatley-on-Thames, 1859
G 49; St 188
Watercolour. 135 × 387 mm
1915–2–13–2 Bequeathed by Mrs Leonora Gillum

View to East from Pompey's Pillar, Alexandria, 1861
Watercolour. 86 × 125 mm
1915–2–13–3 Bequeathed by Mrs Leonora Gillum

The Gibet Mokattam from the Citadel, Cairo, 1861
Watercolour, in artist's mount and frame. 182 × 270 mm
1994–5–14–30 Presented by Mrs Anne E. Christopherson

'Backs of some old houses in Soho', 1866
G 50; St 189
Watercolour. 184 × 189 mm (sight)
1942–10–10–9 Presented by C.F.Bell

'Mr Buckingham's House, Dorchester', 1869
G 51
Watercolour. 263 × 193 mm
1991–10–5–2

John Brett
(1830–1902)

Pansies and Fern-shoots, 1862
G 52
Watercolour, with bodycolour, on card. 153 × 146 mm
1994–5–14–1

Talmage White reading, Capri, 1863
Pencil. 249 × 175 mm
1989–5–13–23

Girl's Head in profile [possibly Georgina Weldon], 1868
Pencil. 271 × 191 mm
1989–5–13–24

Head of a middle-aged Woman
Black chalk. 354 × 256 mm (oval)
1989–5–13–25

Ford Madox Brown
(1821–1893)

A Naked Baby held by a Woman, for *'Take Your Son, Sir'*, 1856
G 53; LB 4
Black chalk and grey wash. 175 × 235 mm (oval)
1894–6–12–7

'The Prisoner of Chillon', for *Poets of the Nineteenth Century (1857)*, 1856
G 54
Pencil. 127 × 95 mm
1939–10–14–146 Purchased from Miss J.Wilde, through the H.L.Florence Fund

The Coat of Many Colours
G 55; LB 1
Pen and black ink. 199 × 205 mm
1893–10–18–2

Elijah and the Widow's Son, for *Dalziel's Bible Gallery (1863)*
G 57; LB 3
Pencil. 247 × 148 mm
1894–6–12–8

A Man's left Forearm, for the painting *Work*, 1861

Verso: Sketch of the upper part of a head (chalk)

G 56

Pencil and grey wash. 235 × 229 mm

1939–10–14–147 Purchased from Miss J. Wilde, through the H. L. Florence Fund

St John, design for a stained glass window (possibly for Bradford Cathedral, 1863)

LB 2

Reed pen and grey ink with wash. 343 × 180 mm

1894–6–12–9

King René's Honeymoon, 1864

LB 5

Cartoon brush drawing in brown, with brown wash. 460 × 310 mm

1894–6–12–10

Edward Burne Jones

(1833–1898)

Cupid finding Psyche, 1866

G 58

Watercolour and bodycolour. 668 × 476 mm

1954–5–8–8 Bequeathed by Cecil French

The Princess Sabra in a Garden, 1865–7

G 59

Pencil. 358 × 198 mm

1954–5–8–9 Bequeathed by Cecil French

The Petition to the King, 1865–7

Pencil and black chalk. 352 × 604 mm

1954–5–8–10 Bequeathed by Cecil French

Princess Sabra drawing the Fatal Lot, 1865–7

Pencil and black chalk. 351 × 605 mm

1954–5–8–11 Bequeathed by Cecil French

Princess Sabra tied to a Tree, 1865–7

Pencil. 351 × 298 mm

1954–5–8–12 Bequeathed by Cecil French

St George fighting the Dragon, 1865–7

G 60

Pencil. 351 × 416 mm

1954–5–8–13 Bequeathed by Cecil French

The Return of St George and the Princess Sabra, 1865–7

G 61

Pencil. 353 × 424 mm

1954–5–8–14 Bequeathed by Cecil French

A kneeling nude Man, holding a Pair of Bellows, study for figure of 'Love' in *Chant d'Amour* c.1868–77

G 62

Pencil. 289 × 187 mm

1954–5–8–16 Bequeathed by Cecil French

A Study for *The Romance of the Rose*, 1874

Pencil. 253 × 141 mm

1967–10–14–51 Bequeathed by Dr E. G. Millar

Study for the head of a Sea Nymph, for the *Perseus* series, 1875

Pencil. 268 × 177 mm

1967–10–14–49 Bequeathed by Dr E. G. Millar

The Annunciation, 1879

G 70

Watercolour and bodycolour, with gold. 522 × 214 mm

1954–5–8–15 Bequeathed by Cecil French

Study of a Head, 1879

Pencil. 201 × 157 mm

1955–7–9–14 Presented by Iolo A. Williams

Study for the Slave in *The Wheel of Fortune*, 1879

Pencil. 272 × 180 mm

1967–10–14–47 Bequeathed by Dr E. G. Millar

Nude study for Andromeda in the *Perseus* series, 1885

Pencil. 273 × 182 mm

1967–10–14–48 Bequeathed by Dr E. G. Millar

Study for the last picture in the *Briar Rose* series, 1886

Pencil. 221 × 270 mm

1955–7–9–13 Presented by Iolo A. Williams

Portrait of Lady Frances Colvin, c.1890

Pencil. 379 × 354 mm

1927–9–3–1 Bequeathed by Sir Sidney Colvin, through the NACF

Study of a head in profile to right, 1894

Red and black chalk on red paper. 337 × 260 mm

1967–10–14–46 Bequeathed by Dr E. G. Millar

A Figure on a Step, design for metal work, 1896

Gold on black prepared paper. 250 × 168 mm

1967–10–14–50 Bequeathed by Dr E. G. Millar

A Woman's Head, in profile to right, 1896

Gold on purple prepared paper. 356 × 250 mm

1901–4–17–20

Study of a Female Figure playing a Musical Instrument, 1897

Gold on purple prepared paper. 301 × 205 mm

1898–7–27–1

Caricatures

Four Figures in long Robes

Pencil, on right half of writing paper. 178 × 225 mm

1941–9–1–5 Presented by Dr Robert Steele

The Turkish Bath (the massage)

Pen and brown ink. 114 × 146 mm

1950–7–10–1 Presented by Mrs Gerald Allingham

The Turkish Bath (man's head in profile)

Pen and brown ink. 37 × 37 mm

1950–7–10–2 Presented by Mrs Gerald Allingham

The Turkish Bath (two men standing)

Pen and brown ink. 113 × 87 mm

1950–7–10–3 Presented by Mrs Gerald Allingham

The Turkish Bath (the massage)

Pen and brown ink. 100 × 115 mm

1950–7–10–4 Presented by Mrs Gerald Allingham

The Turkish Bath (dressing)

Pen and brown ink. 152 × 110 mm

1950–7–10–5 Presented by Mrs Gerald Allingham

Four Designs for Stained Glass Windows for Morris, Marshall, Faulkner & Co. (1861–74) and W. Morris & Co. (1874–1940)

South Transept Window, St Michael and All Angels Church, Lyndhurst, Hampshire, 1863

Pen and grey and brown ink. 346 × 234 mm

1941–12–13–696 Presented by Hermann Burg

Vyner Memorial Window, Lady Chapel, Christ Church Cathedral, Oxford, 1871

Pen and black ink and watercolour. 291 × 207 mm

1941–12–13–697 Presented by Hermann Burg

East Window of Chancel, St Anne's Church, Brown Edge, Staffs., 1873

Pen and black ink and watercolour. 214 × 208 mm

1941–12–13–698 Presented by Hermann Burg

East Window, All Saints, Putney, 1877–8

Pen and watercolour. 250 × 191 mm

1941–12–13–699 Presented by Hermann Burg

Cartoons for 'The Seven Acts of Mercy', circular designs for stained glass windows for St Peter's Church, Bramley, near Leeds, 1874–5

(Not in LB; purchased by the Museum at the artist's sale, Christie's, 18 July 1898, lot 161)

Feeding the Hungry

Pencil. 379 mm dia. (sight)

1898–7–27–2

Giving Drink to the Thirsty

Pencil. 379 mm dia. (sight)

1898–7–27–3

Clothing the Naked

Pencil. 378 mm dia. (sight)

1898–7–27–4

Visiting the Sick

Pencil. 379 mm dia. (sight)

1898–7–27–5

Visiting the Prisoners

Pencil, with red chalk. 368 mm dia. (sight)

1898–7–27–6

Leading the Blind

Pencil. 366 mm dia. (sight)

1898–7–27–7

Teaching the Young

Pencil. 370 mm dia. (sight)

1898–7–27–8

Album: *Caricatures*, by Rossetti and Burne Jones (with some anonymous), mostly of William Morris, *c.*1865–80

G 63–69

Pencil and pen. 330 × 255 mm

1939–5–13–1 to 19(1–9), 20 to 56 Presented by Dr Robert Steele

Album: *The Flower Book*, 42 Watercolours of fanciful or symbolic Designs, all circular, each suggested by an old English vernacular name of a Flower, 1882–98

(* indicates it has been removed from the album and mounted)

album size 325 × 245 mm

1909–5–12–1 (1. . .42) Purchased from the artist's widow

A Facsimile was published by the Fine Art Society in 1905

'Love in a Mist'

Watercolour and bodycolour. 170 × 150 mm (trimmed on sides)

1909–5–12–1(1)

'Goldenthread'

Watercolour and bodycolour. 165 × 155 mm (trimmed on sides)

1909–5–12–1(2)

'Jacob's Ladder'

Watercolour and bodycolour. 154 mm dia.

1909–5–12–1(3)

'Traveller's Joy'

Watercolour and bodycolour. 155 mm dia.

1909–5–12–1(4)

'Rose of Heaven'*

Watercolour and bodycolour, with gold. 156mm dia.

1909–5–12–1(5)

'Flower of God'*

Watercolour and bodycolour, with gold. 159mm dia.

1909–5–12–1(6)

'Earth's Stars'

Pencil sketch. 152mm dia.

1909–5–12–1(7)

'Golden Cup'

Watercolour and bodycolour, with gold. 160mm dia.

1909–5–12–1(8)

'Adder's Tongue'

Watercolour and bodycolour, with gold. 165mm dia.

1909–5–12–1(9)

'Golden Gate'

Watercolour and bodycolour, with gold. 160mm dia.

1909–5–12–1(10)

'Venus' Looking Glass'*

Watercolour and bodycolour, with gold. 155mm dia.

1909–5–12–1(11)

'Key of Spring'*

Watercolour and bodycolour, with gold. 169mm dia.

1909–5–12–1(12)

'Ladder of Heaven'

Watercolour and bodycolour, with gold. 164mm dia.

1909–5–12–1(13)

'Comes He Not'

Watercolour and bodycolour, with gold. 160mm dia.

1909–5–12–1(14)

'Love in a Tangle'*

G 71

Watercolour and bodycolour, with gold. 163mm dia.

1909–5–12–1(15)

'Witche's [sic] Tree'

Watercolour and bodycolour. 170mm dia.

1909–5–12–1(16)

'Grave of the Sea'

Watercolour and bodycolour. 168mm dia.

1909–5–12–1(17)

'Golden Greeting'

Watercolour and bodycolour. 166mm dia.

1909–5–12–1(18)

'Golden Shower'

Watercolour and bodycolour, with gold. 165mm dia.

1909–5–12–1(19)

'Flame Heath'

Watercolour and bodycolour, with gold and silver. 163mm dia.

1909–5–12–1(20)

'Star of Bethlehem'*

Watercolour and bodycolour, with gold and silver. 158 × 158mm

1909–5–12–1(21)

'Morning Glories'

Watercolour and bodycolour, with gold. 165mm dia.

1909–5–12–1(22)

'With the Wind'

Watercolour and bodycolour. 156mm dia.

1909–5–12–1(23)

'Wake Dearest'

Watercolour and bodycolour, with silver. 157mm dia.

1909–5–12–1(24)

'Wall Tryst'

Watercolour and bodycolour. 159mm dia.

1909–5–12–1(25)

'Helen's Tears'*

G 72

Watercolour and bodycolour, with gold. 166mm dia.

1909–5–12–1(26)

'Marvel of the World'*

Watercolour and bodycolour, with gold. 161mm dia.

1909–5–12–1(27)

'Black Arch Angel'*

Watercolour and bodycolour, with gold. 157mm dia.

1909–5–12–1(28)

'Arbor Tristis'*

Watercolour. 158mm dia.

1909–5–12–1(29)

'Scattered Starwort'

Watercolour and bodycolour, with gold and silver. 164mm dia.

1909–5–12–1(30)

'Saturn's Loathing'*

G 73

Watercolour and bodycolour, with gold. 144 × 143mm dia.

1909–5–12–1(31)

'Welcome to the House'

Watercolour and bodycolour, with gold. 160mm dia.

1909–5–12–1(32)

'Honour's Prize'

Watercolour and bodycolour, with gold and silver. 160mm dia.

1909–5–12–1(33)

'Most Bitter Moonseed'

Watercolour and bodycolour, with gold. 160mm dia.

1909–5–12–1(34)

'White Garden'

Watercolour and bodycolour.
157mm dia.

1909–5–12–1(35)

'Meadow Sweet'

Watercolour and bodycolour, with gold.
163mm dia.

1909–5–12–1(36)

'False Mercury'*

Watercolour and bodycolour, with gold.
155mm dia.

1909–5–12–1(37)

'Fire Tree'

Watercolour and bodycolour, with gold.
164mm dia.

1909–5–12–1(38)

Rough Sketches

Pencil. 150mm dia.

1909–5–12–1(39, 40)

'God's Candle'

Pencil. 150mm dia.

1909–5–12–1(41)

'Day and Night'

Watercolour and bodycolour.
160mm dia.

1909–5–12–1(42)

Album: *The Secret Book of Designs*, album of 222 drawings, some related to projects Burne Jones was working on while others are ideas, 1885–9

G 74

Black chalk, coloured chalks, watercolour. 374 × 300mm

1899–7–13–322 to 544 Bequeathed by the artist

Album: *Letters to Katie*, 101 comic drawings and illustrated letters, with envelopes, etc. addressed to Miss Katharine Lewis, 1880s

G 75

Pen and ink and pencil. 392 × 289mm

1960–10–14–2(1. . .101) Presented by Miss Katharine Lewis

Published, with introduction by John Christian, by British Museum Publications in 1988

Album: Studies of Heads, Figures, Armour and Drapery, album of 21 remaining leaves, most with drawings on recto and verso (given to Eric Millar by Angela Thirkell, 1952), 1880s–90s

Pencil. 375 × 265mm

1967–10–14–52(1. . .21) Bequeathed by Dr E. G. Millar

George James Howard, 9th Earl of Carlisle

(1843–1911)

Discus thrower – probationary drawing for Heatherly's Academy, c.1864–6

Pencil. 760 × 435mm

1993–5–8–10

A frenzied Maenad, from a Roman relief in the British Museum

Black and white chalk on blue paper. 444 × 280mm

1993–5–8–17 Presented by Martin and Marlies Royalton-Kisch

Marietta – Rome, c.1865–6

Pencil. 314 × 222mm

1993–5–8–6

Quincerta, 1865–6

Pencil. 335 × 238mm

1993–5–8–6

Sketches of three Italian peasant women, 1865–6

Pencil. 256 × 355mm

1993–5–8–11

Two Ladies under a Pergola below a Cliff

G 76

Watercolour with bodycolour.
365 × 264mm

1953–10–12–2 Presented by J. A. Gere

Frederick Sitwell, Lady Colvin's son by her first marriage, on his deathbed, 1873

Pencil. 169 × 349mm

1927–9–3–2 Bequeathed by Sir Sidney Colvin through the NACF

Minster in Thanet

Watercolour with bodycolour.
171 × 352mm

1912–8–2–1 Presented by Sir Sidney Colvin

View of a headland, c.1883?

Pencil. 146 × 240mm

1993–5–8–9

Portrait of Cecilia Howard, 1891

Pencil. 330 × 228mm

1993–5–8–8

Four portrait sketches of Francis Turner Palgrave, 1895

Pencil. 194 × 126mm each

1941–12–13–496. . .499 Presented by the Reverend Francis and Miss Annora Palgrave

Charles Allston Collins

(1828–1873)

All eighteen works by Collins in the Museum's collection, 1891–4–4–12 to 29 (LB 1 to 12), are discussed in full in the present catalogue (G 77–94).

Walter Crane

(1845–1915)

There are over 250 designs and drawings for book illustrations by Crane in the Museum, which have not been included in the following list.

Portrait of the Artist's Wife at the Grove of Egeria, 1872

Pencil. 328 × 255 mm

1991–10–5–19

A Stream in a Wood, 1874

G 95
Watercolour and bodycolour.
228 × 317 mm

1989–9–30–138

Nude study of girl seated in profile, Rome, 1882

Pencil. 303 × 213 mm

1933–4–11–194

Portrait of E.E.H., wearing dress with frilled collar, 1889

Pencil. 127 × 85 mm

1987–7–25–32 Presented by Miss M. Ball

A Sicilian Idyll, 1890

Pen and black ink. 130 × 108 mm

1933–4–11–214

Henry Holiday

(1839–1927)

Two Women in Sixteenth-Century Costume, for *The Bride and Daughters of Jerusalem*, c.1861–2

G 96
Watercolour and bodycolour.
345 × 203 mm

1982–5–15–22

A Young Man Seated, for an illustration in *Aglaia*

Pencil. 322 × 206 mm

1980–7–26–21

Winifred Raven Holiday, daughter of the artist, aged 10, 1906

Pencil. 180 × 132 mm (inserted in album at 198* a 9)

1952–10–14–1 Presented by Miss Jessie Nethersole

Arthur Hughes

(1832–1915)

A Lady standing by a Sundial

G 97
Pen and brown ink. 93 × 56 mm

1916–11–15–1 Presented by J.P. Heseltine

Home from Work, [c.1861]

G 98
Pen and brown ink. 112 × 84 mm

1916–11–15–2 Presented by Mrs Francis Dodd

'La Belle Dame sans Merci'

G 99
Pen and brown ink. 100 × 59 mm

1916–11–15–3 Presented by Professor Michael E. Sadler

'La Belle Dame sans Merci'

G 100
Pen and brown ink. 83 × 91 mm

1916–11–15–4 Presented by Professor Michael E. Sadler

Design for the frontispiece of Christina Rossetti's *Sing Song*, 1872

Pen and black ink. 155 × 105 mm (image), 257 × 181 mm (sheet)

1937–5–29–1

Two illustrations to Christina Rossetti's *Sing Song* (pages 25 and 46), 1872

Pen and black ink. 254 × 178 mm

1937–5–29–2

Two illustrations to Christina Rossetti's *Sing Song* (pages 110 and 108), 1872

Pen and black ink. 253 × 178 mm

1937–5–29–3

Two illustrations to Christina Rossetti's *Sing Song* (pages 129 and 115), 1872

Pen and grey ink. 257 × 181 mm

1937–5–29–4

William Holman Hunt

(1827–1910)

Valentine rescuing Silvia from Proteus, c.1851

G 1
Pen and black ink. 237 × 321 mm (image), 267 × 366 mm (sheet)

1927–3–12–1 Presented by Mrs Holman Hunt

The Lady of Shalott, c.1856

G 2
Pen and brown ink. 186 × 247 mm

1985–11–9–15

'Lady Clara Vere de Vere', c.1856

G 3
Pen and brown ink. 180 × 114 mm

1992–4–4–23

A Man embracing a Woman, for 'Lady Clara Vere de Vere', c.1856

G 4
Pen and brown ink. 180 × 114 mm

1992–4–4–24

A Man in Eastern Costume, walking to right with a Basket on his Back – study for St Joseph for the first version of *The Triumph of the Innocents*, 1876

G 5

Metal point and pencil. 478 × 297 mm

1927–3–12–2 Presented by Mrs Holman Hunt

Design for stained glass window of Melchisedek

Watercolour, pen and ink, and gold. 424 × 249 mm

1947–7–25–4 Presented by Dudley Snelgrove

John Everett Millais

(1829–1896)

Lorenzo and Isabella, 1848–9

G 37; LB 3

Pencil. 225 × 310 mm

1901–5–16–10

A Lady in a Garden cutting a Flower from a Trellis, for *The Germ*, 1849–50

G 38; LB 4

Pencil, on a fragment of an etching. 288 × 116 mm

1901–5–16–9

The Eve of the Deluge, *c.*1850–1

G 39; LB 2

Pen and Indian ink with wash, squared. 240 × 413 mm

1901–5–16–8

After the Battle

Brush drawing in brown wash. 220 × 288 mm

1937–4–10–6 Presented by L. G. Esmond Morse, in memory of his father, Sidney Morse

Head and Shoulders of a Young Girl: Ann Lynn, 1852

G 40

Watercolour. 220 × 192 mm

1967–10–14–124 Bequeathed by Dr E. G. Millar

Head and Shoulders of a Young Girl: Fanny Lynn, 1853

G 41

Watercolour. 215 × 188 mm

1967–10–14–126 Bequeathed by Dr E. G. Millar

Humorous Drawing: Sporting Gent and Highland Boy, 1853

G 42

Pen and brown ink. 179 × 111 mm

1979–4–7–13

Married for Love, 1853

G 43

Pen and black ink, with grey wash. 246 × 174 mm

1976–10–30–32

'Retribution', 1854

G 44

Pen and brown ink. 201 × 256 mm (image), 214 × 275 mm (sheet)

1982–12–11–1

Sketches for *Peace Concluded*, 1856

G 45; LB 5b

Pencil. 162 × 226 mm

1901–5–16–15

Composition Study for *Peace Concluded*, 1856

G 46; LB 5a

Pencil. 228 × 178 mm

1901–5–16–14

The Good Samaritan, sketch for a wood cut for *The Parables of Our Lord* (1864), 1857

LB 6a

Pen and brown ink. 57 × 53 mm

1901–5–16–11

Study of a donkey, for 'The Good Samaritan', a wood cut for *The Parables of Our Lord* (1864), 1857

LB 6b

Pencil, with pen and brown ink. 152 × 88 mm

1901–5–16–12

The Pearl of Great Price, an illustration for *The Parables of Our Lord* (1864)

LB 1

Pen and grey ink, with watercolour. 158 × 119 mm

1900–4–11–6

'A Lost Love', engraved for *Once a Week* (December, 1859)

G 47

Watercolour. 104 × 85 mm

1937–4–10–3 Presented by L. G. Esmond Morse, in memory of his father, Sydney Morse

The Black Brunswicker (copy of the painting exhibited at the RA, 1860)

Watercolour, heightened with white. 156 × 99 mm

1967–10–14–125 Bequeathed by Dr E. G. Millar

Study for the painting *Jephthah's Daughter* (exhibited at the RA, 1867)

LB 7

Brush drawing in brown wash, squared. 251 × 297 mm

1901–5–16–13

William Henry Millais

(1828–1899)

A Scottish Farmstead

G 101; St 190

Watercolour. 180 × 329 mm

1974–6–15–8

William Morris

(1834–1896)

Head of Jane Burden (Mrs Morris), *c.*1857

Verso: Figure sitting, wearing a toga, with a sword

G 102

Pencil. 104 × 76 mm

1939–6–2–1 Presented by Dr Robert Steele

Design for a woodcut initial 'D', for the Kelmscott Press

Pen and black ink. 90 × 56 mm

1967–10–14–128 Bequeathed by Dr E. G. Millar

Rose Bush Design for the background of a stained glass window

Brush drawing in brown wash, over pencil. 636 × 275 mm

1940–10–12–11 Purchased from Morris & Co. through the H. L. Florence Fund

Fruit Tree Design for the background of a stained glass window

Brush drawing in brown and black, over pencil. 635 × 279 mm

1940–10–12–12 Purchased from Morris & Co. through the H. L. Florence Fund

John William North

(1842–1924)

'Requiescat in Pace', illustration for *Poems* by Jean Ingelow, 1867

Pen and ink, with white. 130 × 100 mm (image)

1992–4–6–86 Robin De Beaumont Gift

'The Four Bridges', illustration for *Poems* by Jean Ingelow, 1867

Pen and ink, with white. 130 × 100 mm (image)

1992–4–6–87 Robin De Beaumont Gift

'Glorious things of Thee are spoken', for *Spirit of Praise*, 1867

Pen and ink, with white. 128 × 103 mm (image)

1992–4–6–88 Robin De Beaumont Gift

Landscape with men ploughing, 1873

Watercolour and bodycolour. 282 × 448 mm

1970–3–7–2

Halsway Court, Somerset, 1865

Watercolour and bodycolour. 330 × 445 mm

1994–7–23–2 Purchased with a contribution from the NACF.

Dante Gabriel Rossetti

(1828–1882)

'The Sleeper', c.1848

G 6; S 29

Pen and black ink, pink bodycolour border. 223 × 118 mm (image), 265 × 173 mm (sheet)

1936–6–8–1

Portrait of Christina Rossetti, c.1848

S 424

Pencil and black chalk. 288 × 215 mm

1937–5–8–31

Head of a Girl, c.1849

G 7; S 544

Black chalk and wash over pencil. 166 × 126 mm

1910–12–10–7 Bequeathed by Colonel W. J. Gillum

Composition study for *Found*, 1853

G 8; S 64B

Pen and brown wash, heightened with white. 205 × 182 mm

1910–12–10–1 Bequeathed by Colonel W. J. Gillum

Hamlet and Ophelia, c.1854

G 9

Pen and brown wash. 258 × 181 mm

1974–4–6–11

Arthur's Tomb, 1855

G 10; S 73

Watercolour. 233 × 374 mm (image), 241 × 382 mm (sheet)

1982–6–19–23

Paolo and Francesca

G 11; S 75A

Pencil. 225 × 167 mm

1981–11–7–17

Miss Siddal standing

G 12; S 497

Pen and brown wash. 135 × 52 mm

1912–11–9–5 Presented by Campbell Dodgson

Miss Siddal in a Basket Chair

G 13; S 498

Pencil. 188 × 153 mm

1954–5–8–3 Bequeathed by Cecil French

Miss Siddal in a Basket Chair

G 14; S 496

Pencil. 177 × 185 mm

1910–12–10–6 Bequeathed by Colonel W. J. Gillum

Miss Siddal in an Armchair

G 15; S 495

Pencil. 184 × 118 mm

1910–12–10–5 Bequeathed by Colonel W. J. Gillum

La Belle Dame sans Merci, mid-1850s

G 16; S 76B

Brush drawing in grey wash over pencil. 432 × 332 mm

1910–12–10–2 Bequeathed by Colonel W. J. Gillum

How Sir Galahad, Sir Bors and Sir Percival received the Sanc Grael; but Sir Percival's Sister died by the Way, 1857

G 17; LB 1; S 94

Pen and brown ink. 249 × 351 mm

1885–6–13–81

Mary Magdalene at the Door of Simon the Pharisee, c.1858

G 18; S 109B

Pen and brown ink with wash. 66 × 61 mm

1912–11–9–4 Presented by Campbell Dodgson.

Writing on the Sand, 1859

G 20; LB 2; S 111; St 191

Watercolour. 263 × 241 mm

1886–6–7–14

My Lady Greensleeves, 1859

G 19; S 113

Watercolour and bodycolour.
311 × 185 mm

1954–5–8–1 Bequeathed by
Cecil French

Cassandra, 1861

G 21; S 127

Pen and black ink. 330 × 464 mm

1910–12–10–4 Bequeathed by Colonel
W. J. Gillum

How Sir Galahad, Sir Bors and Sir
Percival received the Sanc Grael;
but Sir Percival's Sister died by the
Way, c.1864

G 22; S 94A

Pen and brown ink. 251 × 351 mm

1910–12–10–3 Bequeathed by Colonel
W. J. Gillum

Hamlet and Ophelia, c.1865–7

G 23; S 108

Pen and black ink. 308 × 261 mm

1910–12–10–8 Bequeathed by Colonel
W. J. Gillum

A Study of Ellen Smith for *A
Christmas Carol*, 1867

S 195A

Pencil. 412 × 355 mm

1954–5–8–7 Bequeathed by
Cecil French

Grotesque sketches of a Man and a
Dragon, etc.

G 24; S 744

Pencil. 229 × 181 mm

1941–9–1–4 Presented by
Dr Robert Steele

'The Bard and the Petty
Tradesman', 1868

G 25; S 609

Pen and brown ink. 116 × 175 mm

1939–5–13–5 Presented by
Dr Robert Steele

'The M's at Ems', 1869

G 26; S 605

Pen and brown ink. 112 × 179 mm

1939–5–13–1 Presented by
Dr Robert Steele

'The German Lesson', 1869

G 27; S 603

Pen and brown ink. 145 × 178 mm

1939–5–13–2 Presented by
Dr Robert Steele

'Resolution; or, The Infant
Hercules', 1869

G 28; S 604

Pen and brown ink. 205 × 131 mm

1939–5–13–8 Presented by
Dr Robert Steele

Jane Morris leading the Wombat,
1869

G 30; S 607

Pen and brown ink. 179 × 112 mm

1939–5–13–3 Presented by
Dr Robert Steele

Rossetti lamenting the death of his
Wombat, 1869

G 29; S 606

Pen and brown ink and wash.
179 × 112 mm

1939–5–13–6 Presented by
Dr Robert Steele

Mrs Morris on a Sofa, 1870

G 33; S 380

Black chalk and pencil. 343 × 423 mm
(image), 352 × 461 mm (sheet)

1954–5–8–4 Bequeathed by
Cecil French

Study of Mrs Morris, for Beatrice
in *Dante's Dream* (Walker Art
Gallery), 1870

S 81B R1E

Chalks on light green paper.
600 × 511 mm

1954–5–8–6 Bequeathed by
Cecil French

Morris in a Punt, 1871

G 31; S 608

Pen and brown ink. 179 × 112 mm

1939–5–13–9 Presented by
Dr Robert Steele

Mrs Morris on a Sofa, 1872

G34; S 393

Pen and brown ink. 283 × 437 mm

1954–5–8–2 Bequeathed by Cecil
French

The Nun

S 610

Pen and brown ink. 180 × 114 mm

1939–5–13–4 Presented by
Dr Robert Steele

'Rupes Topseia', c.1874

G 32; S 611

Pen and brown ink. 179 × 112 mm

1939–5–13–7 Presented by
Dr Robert Steele

Orpheus and Eurydice in Hades,
with Pluto and Proserpine, 1875

G 36; S 243

Pencil. 610 × 514 mm

1910–12–10–9 Bequeathed by Colonel
W. J. Gillum

Sketch from a classical Statue, 1879

S 612

Pen and brown ink. 180 × 114 mm

1939–5–13–10 Presented by
Dr Robert Steele

Triangular Fashions

(not in S, probably not by Rossetti)

Pen and brown ink. 178 × 112 mm

1939–5–13–11 Presented by
Dr Robert Steele

Half-length Figures of a Man and a
Woman embracing, for *The Blessed
Damozel* (Fogg Art Museum,
Harvard), *c*.1873–7

G 35; S 244J

Pencil, over red chalk. 239 × 290mm

1954–5–8–5 Bequeathed by
Cecil French

Dante relating his dream, study for
the second predella of *Dante's
Dream* (Dundee City Art Gallery),
c.1879

S 81B R2C

Black chalk, on two joined sheets.
484 × 963mm

1910–12–10–10 Bequeathed by Colonel
W.J.Gillum

Figures of Dante and *Love* by a
Well, for *The Salutation of Beatrice*
(Toledo, Ohio), *c*.1880

S 260C

Pencil on buff paper. 380 × 265mm

1910–12–10–11 Bequeathed by Colonel
W.J.Gillum

Album: Album of Caricatures by
Rossetti and Burne Jones (with
some anonymous), mostly of
William Morris, *c*.1865–80

G – 63 to 69

Pen and ink. 330 × 255mm

1939–5–13–1 to 19(1–9), 20 to 56
Presented by Dr Robert Steele (Nos.
1 . . .11 are by Rossetti and have been
given individual entries in this checklist, in
chronological order)

Album: Album of Rossetti material,
34 items, including letters, portraits
(some photographs, including
Ruskin with Rossetti), press
cuttings, early drawing attributed
to Bell Scott and E.J.Hipkins, and
latter's bookplate.

Miscellaneous, as above. 285 × 215mm
(album)

1936–11–19–1(1 . . .34) Presented by
Miss Edith J.Hipkins

John Ruskin

(1819–1900)

Gate of Ancient Palace, Nancy

Pen and grey ink with white, on grey
paper. 330 × 226mm

1901–5–6–2 Presented by
Mrs Arthur Severn

'Near Meillerie, Chillon in the
distance' and 'The Valley of the
Rhône and Bernese Alps', 1833

Pen and grey ink. 344 × 241mm

1901–5–6–3 Presented by
Mrs Arthur Severn

The Castle Rock, St John's Vale,
1838

Pencil, with white, on blue paper.
255 × 362mm

1909–5–29–1 Bequeathed by
Mrs Barton

Pinnacle and arcade, study for
Stones of Venice, *c*.1849

Pencil with brown wash. 193 × 87mm
(irregular)

1906–11–23–3 Presented by
Sidney Colvin

Gable, chimney, tower, etc., studies
for *Stones of Venice*, 1849

Pencil, with watercolour. 251 × 146mm

1906–11–23–4 Presented by
Sidney Colvin

Chamonix, 1850

Pencil, pen and brown ink with wash and
white bodycolour. 516 × 379mm

1944–19–14–168 Presented by Miss
M.H.Turner

The Deluge – sculptured relief on a
spandrel, Bourges Cathedral, 1851

LB 5

Pencil, with white, on blue prepared
paper. 288 × 194mm

1901–5–16–3

Fribourg, Switzerland, 1859

LB 2; St 182

Pen and ink and watercolour, on
blue-grey paper. 225 × 288mm

1901–5–16–4

The Towers of Fribourg, *c*.1859

Watercolour. 284 209mm

1985–10–5–1

A Rock covered with Ivy and
Lichen, *c*.1872

G 104

Watercolour, with bodycolour.
400 × 270mm (image), 455 × 346mm
(sheet)

1979–1–27–11

Etna from Taormina, 1874

Watercolour with bodycolour.
170 × 249mm

1931–6–18–1

Mont Salève, *c*.1879

Watercolour and pencil, with white, on
buff paper. 182 × 126mm

1931–5–29–2 Presented by Messrs
Stevens and Brown

Valley of the Arve from above
Bonneville, 1879

Watercolour and pencil. 119 × 234mm

1931–5–29–3 Presented by Messrs
Stevens and Brown

Flowers, 'done to amuse "Sophie"
at the Thwaite', 1886

Watercolour, with white, on blue-grey
paper. 126 × 175mm

1946–10–12–6, 7

**The following works by Ruskin are
undated and given in Register
number order:**

Study of a Dead Wild Duck

LB 6

Watercolour. 331 × 532mm

1901–5–16–1

Two detached Columns in the Vestibule of St Mark's, Venice

LB 4

Watercolour with white, on purple paper

1901–5–16–2

At Interlaken, Switzerland

LB 1

Bodycolour, on green-grey paper.
215 × 329 mm

1901–5–16–5

View near Verona, view over plain

LB 3a

Pencil on buff paper

1901–5–16–6

View near Verona, view from hillside

LB 3b

Pencil, with white, on grey paper.
176 × 263 mm

1901–5–16–7

The Jura, Hill of Habsburg, and Valley of the Aare

Watercolour, with white, on grey paper.
134 × 214 mm

1931–6–18–2

Monte Viso, going from Turin to Genoa

Pencil and watercolour. 122 × 198 mm

1931–6–18–3

Venetian balcony

Brush drawing in grey wash, with pencil.
119 × 186 mm

1944–10–14–169 Presented by
Miss M. H. Turner

Study of a Snake

Watercolour, with white, on buff paper.
109 × 155 mm

1944–10–14–170 Presented by
Miss M. H. Turner

Mountains and a lake

Watercolour over pencil. 150 × 148 mm

1946–10–12–2

Mountains and a lake, with castle

Watercolour over pencil. 145 × 163 mm

1946–10–12–3

Amiens Cathedral

Watercolour with bodycolour.
149 × 225 mm

1946–10–12–4

The Campanile, Piazza San Marco, Venice

Watercolour, with white, on grey paper.
163 × 126 mm

1946–10–12–5

St Jean d'Acre Pillar, Venice

Watercolour, with white, on purple paper.
280 × 222 mm

1967–10–14–141 Bequeathed by
Dr E. G. Millar

Frederick Sandys

(1829–1904)

Copy of a Raphael drawing of the group of mathematicians in *The School of Athens*

Pen and brown ink, over pencil, on brown paper. 251 × 335 mm

1947–4–12–159

Greenhithe

LB 1

Pencil, with white, on grey paper.
239 × 351 mm

1875–8–14–1186

The Damosel of the San Graal

Black and red chalk, with white, on green paper. 655 × 479 mm

1940–4–13–84 Presented by
C. Davies Sherborn

Phryne, 1860

Verso: Three Figure Studies

Pencil. 273 × 202 mm

1910–10–13–27 Purchased from
Mrs Sandys

Ruth Herbert, 1860

G 105

Black and white chalk, on buff paper.
409 × 160 mm

1910–10–13–25 Purchased from
Mrs Sandys

Study of a Woman's Head, in profile to left, 1860

Black, red and white chalk, on buff paper.
230 × 177 mm

1910–10–13–26 Purchased from
Mrs Sandys

Sketch of a Woman's face in profile to left

Pencil. 64 × 56 mm

1910–10–13–29 Purchased from
Mrs Sandys

Three Sketches of a Woman to illustrate 'Manoli' in *Cornhill Magazine*, 1861

Pencil. 63 × 100 mm

1910–10–13–30 Purchased from
Mrs Sandys

Studies for the Skeleton and the Woman in 'Until her Death', for *Good Words*, 1862

Pencil. 150 × 178 mm

1949–4–11–39, 40 Bequeathed by
Campbell Dodgson

Two Studies for an illustration of 'The Waiting Time', 1863

Pencil. 62 × 127 mm and 186 × 122 mm

1927–4–19–2, 3

Two sketches for an illustration to Christina Rossetti's 'Amor Mundi' for *Shilling Magazine*, 1865

Pencil. 66 × 107 mm

1910–10–13–29 Purchased from
Mrs Sandys

Jacob at Beersheba, for *Dalziel's Bible Gallery*, 1880

Pen and black ink. 228 × 158 mm

1935–7–16–2 Purchased from
Colnaghi's through H. L. Florence Fund

William Bell Scott

(1811–1890)

A Procession of Young Women carrying hearts to Lady seated by a trellis on a hill in a landscape

Pen and ink, on folded sheet with verse inside. 232 × 190 mm

1936–11–9–1(6) Presented by Miss Edith J. Hipkins (bound in Album of Rossetti material)

Interior with a Man and a Woman embracing on a Sofa, 1863

G 106

Brush drawing in brown, red and black wash, with white. 124 × 172 mm

1974–6–15–7

Waves breaking on a Shore, 1864

Watercolour, with bodycolour. 196 × 343 mm

1983–10–1–17

King Edward's Bay, Tynemouth

G 107; St 178

Watercolour, with bodycolour. 251 × 353 mm

1954–3–2–1 Presented by J. A. Gere

Arthur Severn

(1831–1904)

Gordale Scar, Yorkshire, 1877

G 108

Watercolour. 247 × 352 mm

1988–4–9–3

Fir Island, Coniston Lake

Watercolour. 236 × 366 mm

1938–12–22–1 Purchased through the H. L. Florence Fund

Elizabeth Siddal

(1834–1862)

a. Roundel of an Angel holding Cymbals
b. A Woman with Arms outstretched looking out of a Window

G 109; a. S 699

a. Pencil. b. Pen and brown wash over pencil. 181 × 229 mm

1941–9–1–1 Presented by Dr Robert Steele

a. Sketch of a Figure turned to the left, with another Figure behind
b. Roundel of an Angel holding Cymbals

G 110; S 699A

a. Pencil. b. Pen and brown wash. 181 × 227 mm

1941–9–1–2 Presented by Dr Robert Steele

Sketch of an Angel holding Cymbals

G 111; S 699B

Pencil. 181 × 114 mm

1941–9–1–3 Presented by Dr Robert Steele

James Smetham

(1821–1889)

Portrait of James Griffin, Saddler, of Mare Street, Hackney, 1855

Pen and ink. 148 × 202 mm

1977–4–2–7 Presented by Frances Carey and David Bindman

A Knight kneeling before an Altar (The Knight's Bridal?), 1865

G 112

Watercolour. 289 × 253 mm

1977–4–2–3

Paris and Oenone

Brush drawing in brown, with white. 106 × 151 mm

1949–7–23–1 Presented by Lt.-Col. W. E. Moss

Simeon Solomon

(1840–1905)

A Kneeling Bearded Man – study for *The Purification of Isaiah*, 1860

G 113

Pencil and brown wash. 90 × 101 mm

1954–5–8–20 Bequeathed by Cecil French

A Nude Youth and an Old Man – study for *Ezekiel and the Angel*, 1861

Verso: Landscape of Scottish Castle, with water beyond (watercolour)

G 114

Pencil, with pen and brown ink and wash. 229 × 104 mm

1954–5–8–19 Bequeathed by Cecil French

The Painter's Pleasaunce, c.1865

G 115

Watercolour. 120 × 133 mm

1954–5–8–17 Bequeathed by Cecil French

Amoris Sacramentum, 1868

G 116

Pencil, with some pen and ink and watercolour. 335 × 200 mm

1922–4–8–1 Presented by C. H. V. Bancalari

Portrait of a Young Boy, 1868

Black and red chalk. 366 × 293 mm

1908–5–11–1 Presented by Sidney Colvin

'Until the day break and the shadows flee away', 1869

Pencil and black chalk, with bodycolour. 129 × 154 mm

1954–5–8–18 Bequeathed by Cecil French

Study of a Head

Pencil. 242 × 190 mm

1941–11–4–11 Presented by Professor Basil Williams

Two Cupids meeting, design for tail-piece of Vol. IV of *Hobby Horse*

Pen and blue ink. 80 × 105 mm (in album at 200.c.2)

1896–10–19–128 Presented by Herbert Horne

Frederick Walker

(1840–1875)

Sketch portrait of Frank Nowlan at Leigh's School of Art, 1858

Pencil. 116 × 95 mm

1911–8–21–1 Presented by Frank Nowlan

Unfinished sketch for 'The Settlers of Long Arrow' for *Once a Week*, 1861

LB 1

Watercolour. 119 × 144 mm

1893–8–4–1 Presented by T. Ballard

Sketch for 'Strange Faces', 1862

Pencil with grey wash. 488 × 633 mm

1920–10–12–5

The Spring of Life; or In an Orchard, 1866

Watercolour and bodycolour. 268 × 221 mm

1954–5–8–22 Bequeathed by Cecil French

The Milkmaid

Watercolour. 174 × 81 mm

1936–4–10–8

An Amateur; or Coachman and Cabbage, 1870

G 117; St 194

Watercolour. 177 × 252 mm

1954–5–8–21 Bequeathed by Cecil French

'The Escape', illustrated in *Once a Week*, 1871

Watercolour and bodycolour. 158 × 254 mm

1967–10–14–158 Bequeathed by Dr E. G. Millar

The First Swallow

Watercolour and bodycolour. 352 × 239 mm

1954–5–8–23 Bequeathed by Cecil French

The Secret

Brush drawing in grey wash, over pencil. 120 × 150 mm

1937–4–10–7

Lady arranging Flowers

Pen and brown ink on blue paper. 195 × 155 mm

1953–4–11–38 Bequeathed by E. H. W. Meyerstein

Thomas Woolner

(1825–1892)

A Shepherd Boy with his dog, playing a pipe – design for the vignette on the title-page of F. T. Palgrave's *Golden Treasury* (1861)

G 48

Pencil. 266 × 176 mm

1941–12–13–527 Presented by the Reverend Francis and Miss Palgrave

(attr. to Woolner) Design for a relief of 'The Fall of Man' for decorations in spandrels above an ogee arch

Verso: Standing Woman with Child

Pencil. 185 × 225 mm

1941–12–13–528 Presented by the Reverend Francis and Miss Palgrave

Bibliography and Abbreviations

Literature

Bennett, Merseyside Colls. Cat., 1988

Mary Bennett, *Artists of the Pre-Raphaelite Circle: The First Generation. Catalogue of Works in the Walker Art Gallery, Lady Lever Art Gallery and Sudley Art Gallery, Liverpool* (National Museums and Galleries on Merseyside, 1988)

Bryson and Troxell

John Bryson and Janet Camp Troxell, *Dante Gabriel Rossetti and Jane Morris: Their Correspondence* (Oxford, 1974)

Grieve

Alistair Grieve, *The Art of Dante Gabriel Rossetti: 1. Found. 2. The Pre-Raphaelite Modern-Life Subject* (Norwich, 1976)

Hueffer

Ford Madox Hueffer, *Ford Madox Brown: A Record of his Life and Work* (1896)

Ironside and Gere

Robin Ironside and John Gere, *Pre-Raphaelite Painters* (1948)

J. G. Millais

John Guille Millais, *The Life and Letters of Sir John Everett Millais*, 2 vols. (1899)

LB

Laurence Binyon, *Catalogue of Drawings by British Artists in the Department of Prints and Drawings in the British Museum*, 4 vols. (1898–1907)

M *or* Marillier

H. C. Marillier, *Dante Gabriel Rossetti: An Illustrated Memorial of His Art and Life* (1899)

Newman and Watkinson

Teresa Newman and Roy Watkinson, *Ford Madox Brown and the Pre-Raphaelite Circle* (1991)

Pre-Raphaelite Journal

William E. Fredeman, ed., *The PRB Journal, William Michael Rossetti's Diary of the Pre-Raphaelite Brotherhood 1849–1853* (Oxford, 1975)

Pre-Raphaelitism

William Holman Hunt, *Pre-Raphaelitism and the Pre-Raphaelite Brotherhood*, 2nd ed. revised by M.E.Holman Hunt, 2 vols. (1913)

Rossetti *Letters*

Oswald Doughty and John Robert Wahl, eds., *Letters of Dante Gabriel Rossetti*, 4 vols. (Oxford, 1965–7)

W.M.Rossetti DGR as D&W

William M.Rossetti, *Dante Gabriel Rossetti as Designer and Writer* (1889)

W.M.Rossetti L&L

William M. Rossetti, *Dante Gabriel Rossetti: His Family Letters with a Memoir*, 2 vols. (1895)

Ruskin *Works*

John Ruskin *Works*, E.T.Cook and A.Wedderburn, eds., 39 vols (1903–12)

Staley

Allen Staley, *The Pre-Raphaelite Landscape* (Oxford, 1973)

S *or* Surtees

Virginia Surtees, *The Paintings and Drawings of Dante Gabriel Rossetti (1828–1882). A Catalogue Raisonné*, 2 vols. (Oxford, 1971)

Surtees *Madox Brown*

Virginia Surtees, ed., *Diary of Ford Madox Brown* (New Haven and London 1981)

Exhibitions

Boyce Exh., Tate 1987

George Price Boyce, Tate Gallery, 1987. Catalogue by Christopher Newall and Judy Egerton

St *or* British Landscape Watercolours Exh., BM 1985

British Landscape Watercolours 1600–1860, British Museum, 1985. Catalogue by Lindsay Stainton

Burne-Jones Exh., Arts Council 1975

The Paintings, Graphic and Decorative Work of Sir Edward Burne-Jones 1833–98, Arts Council Exh., Hayward Gallery, London, Southampton Art Gallery, City Museum and Art Gallery, Birmingham, 1975–76. Catalogue by John Christian

Holman Hunt Exh., Liverpool 1969

William Holman Hunt, Walker Art Gallery, Liverpool, and Victoria and Albert Museum, 1969. Catalogue by Mary Bennett

Millais Drawings Exh., Arts Council 1979

The Drawings of John Everett Millais, Arts Council touring exhibition (Bolton, Brighton, Sheffield, Cambridge, Cardiff) 1979. Catalogue by Malcolm Warner

Millais Exh., RA 1967

Millais, Royal Academy, and Walker Art Gallery, Liverpool, 1967. Catalogue by Mary Bennett

Nature into Art Exh., BM 1991

Nature into Art: English Landscape Watercolours from the British Museum, loan exh. to Cleveland Museum of Art, Ohio and North Carolina Museum of Art, Raleigh, 1991 (N. Carolina and BMP). Catalogue by Lindsay Stainton

Rossetti Exh., RA 1973

Dante Gabriel Rossetti, Painter and Poet, Royal Academy, and City Museum and Art Gallery, Birmingham, 1973. Catalogue by Virginia Surtees

Tate Exh., 1984

The Pre-Raphaelites, Tate Gallery, 1984 (Tate Gallery and Penguin Books). Intro. by Alan Bowness, catalogue by various